$elling with Intention

2nd Edition

The Mindset and Tools
You Need to Double or
Triple Your Sales This Year!

Ursula C. Mentjes

NEW YORK

$elling with Intention 2nd Edition
The Mindset and Tools You Need to
Double or Triple Your Sales This Year!

by Ursula C. Mentjes
© 2011 Ursula C. Mentjes. All rights reserved.

ISBN 978-1-60037-841-6 (paperback)

ISBN 978-1-60037-842-3 (Epub)

Library of Congree Control Number: 2010933634

Published by:

MORGAN JAMES PUBLISHING
The Entrepreneurial Publisher
5 Penn Plaza, 23rd Floor
New York City, New York 10001
(212) 655-5470 Office
(516) 908-4496 Fax
www.MorganJamesPublishing.com

Interior Design by:
Bonnie Bushman
bbushman@bresnan.net

Dedicated to all Sales
Professionals and Entrepreneurs.

Your fearlessness inspires me every day.

Acknowledgments

*L*ike the many other books that have come before Selling With Intention, this book would not have been possible without the special people who have inspired and mentored me throughout my career and those who offered their amazing talents throughout the writing process.

First and foremost, I want to thank God for the words He gave me to write this book. Through Him, all things are possible.

I want to thank my wonderful husband Tim Bartram who was right about the title (and right about so many other things in the book!). Thank you for all of your brilliant ideas and your willingness to listen whenever I needed to talk things through. Your belief in me and your unending support have enabled me to dream bigger than I ever thought possible. I also want to thank my wonderful family members who have always believed in me. Deep gratitude goes to my parents, dear siblings, Tim's family, and extended family who truly know what it means to give unconditional love. A special Thank You, also, to the Jordahl and Budin families — you are the additional family members that God blessed me with! Finally, to our California family the Ghods, we are eternally grateful for all of your incredible love and support.

You cannot write a book without excellent editors! Alisa Griffis, Write Well, Write Now USA, is an incredibly talented editor and truly helped me mold and shape the First Edition of Selling With Intention. A very special Thank You, also, to Amanda Johnson, True to Intention, for being there to assist me with her expertise in the Second Edition of Selling With Intention. You are a joy to work with, and you always make the process easy and seamless! The original book covers were created by Marcy Decato, Creative Solutions, who is a supremely talented graphics artist and makes every one of her creations perfect!

A gratitude-filled Thank You to all of my dear friends, business associates and strategic referral partners at the numerous organizations that I have been or am a member of. Your extra support has made all of the difference! Thank you...Janise Graham, Gwen Thibeaux, Marisa Arriet, Eydie Stumpf, Peggy Ricks, Michelle Odlund, Laura Bruno, Molly Luffy, and Kendra Brodin.

Special acknowledgment also goes out to The Freedom Circle Mastermind Group, an immensely gifted group of Conscious Entrepreneurs, and our coach Christine Kloser. Your support meant so much during the writing of the Second Edition. Thank you!

Finally, my greatest Thank You goes to my clients — My Sales Coach Now Members, Sales Coach Now Quantum Leap Members, 3-Day Selling With Intention Intensive Participants, etc. — who inspired me to write the Second Edition. I am so blessed to work with such talented people! Thank you for teaching me how to become a better Sales Coach — and person.

Rave Reviews

Selling With Intention is filled with practical and inspirational insights that will help you completely transform your relationship to selling, and yourself as a sales person. Ursula Mentjes knows exactly how to guide any sales person to experience more success, more fulfillment and a lot more sales.

Christine Kloser
Best-Selling Author of The Freedom Formula

Selling With Intention is the perfect book for anyone who wants to sell, influence, persuade, or communicate. In other words: Anyone in business. Author Ursula Mentjes gives you the skills and confidence to sell with integrity and intention.

Libby Gill
Best-Selling Author of *You Unstuck*

The key to success in business is sales: Selling you, selling your product, and selling your service. No book can teach you selling more clearly than *Selling With Intention*. If it is your intention to grow your business, then you must buy this book today!

Liz Goodgold
Author of *Red Fire Branding:*
Creating a Hot Personal Brand to Have Customers For Life

$elling with Intention

You can spend many years and many tens of thousands of dollars on programs that teach you how to sell. But if selling conflicts with your values and authenticity, you can't win. Either you "sell" out your soul, or you starve. Ursula Mentjes dissolves that conflict instantly and elegantly with *Selling With Intention*. Selling effectively becomes effortless.

Morgana Rae
Author of *Financial Alchemy:*
Twelve Months of Magic and Manifestation

Selling With Intention offers a dynamic blueprint and action plan guaranteed to take your business to the next level. Follow the ten principles and exercises, and you cannot fail.

Susan Levin
Founder of Speaker Services, Inc.

Selling With Intention demystifies selling and takes you through an effective process of eliminating the subconscious beliefs that prevent you from excelling. With its principles and intentional actions, *Selling With Intention* is a practical, no-nonsense guide to unlocking your sales potential. If you are ready to take your sales to another level, Selling With Intention is the book to read!

Gwen Thibeaux
Author of *Embracing the Greatness Within:*
A Journey of Purpose and Passion

Having been a corporate consultant in sales training for many years at companies such as Sears Roebuck, J.C. Penney, Stein Mart, Jenny Craig International, and others, I was extremely impressed by Ursula Mentjes's book *Selling With Intention*. It is unique in that it not only sets forth understandable and powerful sales principles, but it addresses another vital aspect of Super Successful Selling — that being the great importance of the Inner Preparation and Consciousness of the Sales person mentally, visually, emotionally, and their expectancy and focus upon and sensitivity to the wants and needs of their clients. This book is a cutting-edge presentation of the exact Sales Process needed in our present ultra-competitive selling environment and a must have for those in the "Selling Game" who want to be Super Successful! You really can't afford to be without it!

Dr. A. Gordon Ray
Author of *Pools In Parched Ground* and
Escalator To The High Life Zone

"I loved this book! It isn't just another sales book, and I have read a lot of them. It's one of the best I have read in a very long time – a great read full of great ideas and wisdom. I have been in sales for most of my life, and I love Ursula's approach. It is cutting edge and will change the way you sell and the way you approach sales in an extremely positive way. If books were keys, this book would be the key to open the door to your success!"

Mitch Mortimer
President and Co-Founder of Author Source Inc.

Selling With Intention is a fun and easy book to read. It is packed with actionable recommendations that can be utilized to substantially increase the success of any business. Ursula's Intentional 30-Second Introduction strategy is nothing short of remarkable.

Dave Gunderson
President and CEO, Credit Union of Southern California

Table of Contents

PART I
SELLING WITH INTENTION

PART II
SPECIAL BONUS SECTION

Introduction

I decided to write *Selling With Intention* after founding my own coaching and consulting company and realizing that many people over-complicate sales. The truth is that sales can be boiled down to a few fundamental principles that are easily followed by a new sales person or by seasoned veterans looking to double or triple their sales!

Throughout my career, I have heard many people saying, "Selling is *difficult*." This includes sales people, sales managers, branch managers, executive managers, and business owners. You have probably heard it too. Let me let you in on a little secret…

Selling is as easy as you make it.

For those who believe selling is difficult, it is. For those who believe selling is easy, it is. Would you like to begin to make selling easier for yourself?

Now, let me draw a sharp distinction: Selling is not *simple*, but I do believe that it can become *easy*. I think, like anything else, that selling is easy if one has the right knowledge. For example, being a dentist would be difficult without the right knowledge about teeth and everything that is involved with dental work. Likewise, being a highly paid and successful sales person will be difficult if you do not have the right knowledge.

So, what is the right knowledge? There are many, many excellent sales training programs in existence that will tell you *how* to make a sale. Those programs will give you the nuts and bolts of the mechanics behind making the sale, such as: Asking closing questions, waiting until the prospect speaks first, isolating objections, and so on. Those courses will likely teach you to be consistent in your sales process to ensure that sales are closed. However, in addition to teaching many techniques and methods that don't feel authentic or natural to most people, these programs leave out essential information on how to sell easily and successfully *with intention.*

I hope you are getting excited about the possibility that increasing your volume and number of sales could actually be easy for you! Believing in that possibility is the first step toward making it a reality.

This book is designed to help you make selling easy by changing the way you *think* about selling. If it is true that we create our own reality, then it is possible to create a reality that includes a world where selling is uncomplicated and easy. The goal of *Selling With Intention* is to help you tap into your subconscious mind and make real changes toward success, and in order to make real change in your life and your sales, you must first develop a clear awareness of how you are holding yourself back.

For those of you who are serious about dramatically impacting your sales results and your bottom line, I have added a Bonus Section to this Second Edition in which I share a few more principles that will help you take a quantum leap in your sales this next year. Enjoy! And be sure to complete all of the "Intentional Action" exercises included in the book.

$ INTENTIONAL ACTION

Complete the exercises along the way so that at the end of this book, you will have created the Intentional Sales Plan that will help you reach your greatest sales goals.

For best results as you read through this book, use the *Selling With Intention* workbook, which is available with other sales training resources at *www.SalesCoachNow.com* and *www.MySalesCoachNow.com*.

If you would like to receive 30 days free on *My Sales Coach Now*, our virtual sales training and coaching community, just e-mail us at *Contact@SalesCoachNow.com* with "30 Days Free" in the subject line, and we'll make that happen for you!

Get ready to change the way you think about selling and double or triple your sales this year!

Blessings on Your Journey,

Ursula Mentjes

Ursula C. Mentjes, M.S., ACC
"The Sales Coach"
Sales Coach Now
Contact@SalesCoachNow.com
www.SalesCoachNow.com
www.MySalesCoachNow.com

PART I

SECOND EDITION

Selling With Intention

Discover How You *Already* Sell With Intention

"He can who thinks he can, and he can't who thinks he can't. This is an inexorable, indisputable law."

— Henry Ford —

You Already Sell With Intention

*T*hat's right! You read the chapter title correctly — you *already* sell with intention, but it might not be in a way that is helping you increase your sales or client base. What does it mean to sell with intention? It means that *you determine the result you want to achieve with a prospect before you even meet with them.* Intention is defined as *"an act or instance of determining mentally upon some action or result"* according to the *American Heritage Dictionary.* Most sales people do have goals for each interaction with a prospect (to move them through the sales process), but they aren't aware of the conflicting intentions, fears, and negative beliefs that their subconscious uses to achieve those goals.

Intention means that you decide *"to act in a specific way"* that gets results. To sell with intention, you make the decision that you are going to *"act a specific way"* and determine the results you want to achieve before you ever meet with the prospect. To make this happen, you must first change your thoughts about what selling means, and then your behavior toward your clients will begin to change. Once your behavior begins to change, then your sales results will begin to change. If you are not clear about the outcome you desire *before* you meet with the client, it is very likely that you will get an outcome that you did not consciously want. By the end of this book, you will not only be able to more accurately determine the result you will achieve with a client *before* you meet with them, you will have the mindset and tools you need to get your intended results almost every time.

To fully understand the power of selling with intention, it is important to examine the simple power of intention. Being intentional and setting your intention can be extremely powerful in your life and in your sales. I teach all of my clients to set their intention, or know their desired result, before they meet with a prospect or make a decision in their personal life. I encourage them, and I would encourage you, to experiment with setting your intention on a daily basis so you can experience the power of being intentional.

The power of intention has played out in my business and in my life many times. One of my favorite memories in business was made at a networking event when the time came for the door prize drawings. I leaned forward to the six women who were sitting at my table and said, "Let's all set our intention that we are going to win!" I remember that they looked at me a little baffled, and then said, "Okay." I'm sure they figured I was a little crazy, but they realized that they had nothing to lose. The first name was drawn. A deep inhale in at our table, and then the name of the woman to my right was called. Our table erupted in clapping as we all smiled and shared knowing glances.

Another name was called, and it turned out to be the woman seated directly across the table from the woman who had just won. Again, we all smiled and clapped and the drawings went on. A couple of women at other tables won and then the next four names picked were those of women at our table! Everyone at our table had won a prize! The women were ecstatic and looked at each other in disbelief. I knew that the power of intention had been at play. So if being intentional can have such amazing results during a door prize drawing, imagine how selling with intention could dramatically increase your results. How intentional have you been in your sales efforts?

One way to bring this conscious level of being into your life and business is to set your intention, specifically with each prospect on your target client list. Setting your intention means that you are clear each day on what you want to accomplish in those 24 hours, from how you want to start and end your day (meditation, prayer, exercise, etc.) to which prospects you are going to call.

I had the privilege of attending the NLP Institute of California's NLP Certified Coach program. NLP, or Neuro-Linguistic Programming, is an innovative

> To sell with intention, you make the decision that you are going to *"act a specific way"* and determine the results you want to achieve before you ever meet with the prospect!

field that pre-supposes that human beings perceive their own reality and have the ability to influence that reality. This is achieved by tuning into the conscious and subconscious beliefs about their experiences and current life situation. By becoming aware of the inner world, human beings have the power to achieve great things in their lives and businesses. *Selling With Intention* is based on these concepts; they are at the core of this book and the exercises you will be asked to do.

$elling with Intention

Change can only come after awareness has been achieved, and the desire and decision to change has been put into motion. Throughout this book, you will have the opportunity to make real changes regarding how you think about yourself and what you think about selling. The results that you get will be determined by how willing you are to participate in this new way of thinking.

The Universal Laws

Today there is a lot of talk about the Universal Laws and the idea of "attracting" success to you versus just trudging your way through goal-setting. One of the most important laws discussed is the Law of Attraction itself. Simply stated, *like attracts like* in the world of science. When applied to business and sales, sales people attract the clients and circumstances they focus on most.

Whatever you are thinking about is what you will create. Sometimes we convince ourselves that we are thinking about our goals, focusing on them and saying

> Most of the time, we get what we expect, so expect that your prospects will turn into your clients!

positive affirmations. However, if there is an ounce of doubt lingering somewhere in your heart or in your mind, the doubt will manifest itself. Whatever you are worrying about or wherever you are stuck is what you will attract. For example, if you focus your attention on losing your prospect, and that is all you think about, you may unconsciously create that reality.

I recently had a conversation with a client I have known for awhile. She was selling a new product and really struggling with getting clients to keep their appointments.

Because I understand that it is critical that we pay attention to what we are thinking about at all times, especially when we are thinking about our prospects or current clients, I allowed my client to talk through how she was feeling about the new products she was selling and the clients that could really benefit.

We discovered together that she had lost her confidence and was beginning to believe that no one wanted what she was selling. When I helped her reconnect (in her mind) with all of the satisfied clients she already had, she was able to easily shift back into a place of *selling with intention* and *expecting* the prospect to turn into a client. And as soon as she shifted her thoughts, and began to feel better, her experience started to change. Her prospects began keeping their appointments.

So many times we want to blame the clients for not keeping the appointments; but often, they are reflecting exactly *where we are*. In other words, if there is any part of you that doesn't believe you deserve more clients, or if you have limiting beliefs about money and how much you are allowing in, it will likely show up by clients cancelling on you.

I know that might sound strange, but if you think about it, I am sure you will find examples in your own life and business where this has occurred. Most of the time, we get what we expect, so *expect* that your prospects will turn into your clients!

As human beings, we must work very hard to cleanse our minds, on a moment-by-moment basis, of negative thoughts or feelings. This is not easy to do, but it is possible if you are conscious and committed to making this change in your life. When you do this, and focus on what it is you want and what you are committed to achieving, you might just double or triple your sales!

Some people might experience mystical feelings or a sense of Divine intervention. But no matter what, do not doubt the power of the Law of Attraction. Sometimes when wonderful things are happening and flowing in their lives, people begin to doubt that they have anything to do with it. This is the worst trap that you can fall into because it means that you doubt the power of your own mind and your ability to create positive outcomes in your life. Guard your thought world carefully by paying attention to what you are saying to yourself, who you spend your time with, where you spend your time, and what is going on in your head and in your heart in general.

Think of a time when you set a goal and suddenly the right people or opportunities just seemed to "show up". That's because you were extremely clear on your goals and you were attracting those opportunities or people to you! You also believed that you could reach that goal, in your heart as well as your mind, so it happened easily.

When I began growing my first company, I made a conscious effort to continuously apply the Law of Attraction. Early in my business, I decided to add another $10,000 in revenue, and my goal was to have that happen in one month. Without putting any judgment on that goal, I just focused on the $10,000 and stayed open to where and how it would show up. Within thirty days, an opportunity arrived that was almost exactly $10,000 per month! It wasn't exactly the opportunity I had imagined, but it fulfilled my intention.

> Give yourself permission to reach your dreams and goals. When you do this, you will begin to identify any lingering limiting beliefs or thoughts that might have been holding you back. Let them go!

Make Your Head Match Your Heart

My clients frequently remind me of the importance of being aware of our thoughts and intentions. Recently, I had a meeting with one of my long-term business associates. We were in the middle of our conversation when he said to me, "You know, I set my intention pretty clearly at the beginning of the week, but then I realized that even though my intention was in my head, it didn't match what was in my heart."

I asked him to elaborate, and he went on to explain that as a Realtor, he often works weekends. The past weekend had been unusually long and arduous, and even though his intention was to have his phone ringing off the hook on Monday and Tuesday so he could get some of his homes into escrow, what he really wanted in his heart was a break, some time off, a few days to rest and recuperate from a long weekend. So, on Monday and Tuesday, he said his phone didn't ring at all, and he enjoyed a few days off.

On Wednesday, he decided that he was ready to face the world and his clients again. He was clear on his goals and his intention, he said, both in his head AND in his heart. This time, he was happy to say, his phone began ringing off the hook all day Wednesday and had not stopped ringing even as we were meeting. When our chat was over, he checked his messages and told me that he had four missed calls, two messages, and an offer on one of his homes. All because he was clear about what he wanted in his head *and* in his heart. During future sessions, he began to refer to this phenomenon as "turning his faucet on and off". Whenever he is having a dry spell, he simply visualizes turning his faucet back on, and then the deals begin to roll in!

As some of you read this, you are nodding your heads. Yes! This is exactly what has happened to you in the past. Others might be a little more skeptical. How can agreement with our head and our heart magically make the phone ring? The reality is that we have much more control over what happens in our sales careers and businesses than we even realize. The key is to stay tuned in to what is going on in our hearts and minds and listen. My business associate was right. Setting intentions is great — a great place to begin — but if it doesn't match what is going on in your heart, then you might not end up with what you thought you wanted. Once your heart and head agree, then amazing things can happen.

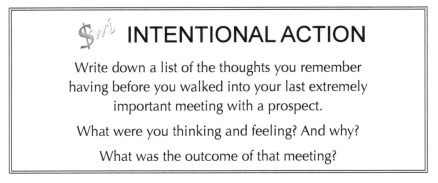

INTENTIONAL ACTION

Write down a list of the thoughts you remember having before you walked into your last extremely important meeting with a prospect.

What were you thinking and feeling? And why?

What was the outcome of that meeting?

Negative Self-Talk and Subconscious Beliefs

Let's examine what is going on inside of our heads. Our subconscious thoughts and beliefs control what we do and how we do it. Our behavior is a result of our subconscious thoughts and beliefs. If you cannot begin to tune into what you are really telling yourself, then you will stay exactly where you are. For example, if we were having a conversation right now at this very moment, you might share things with me that you know are true about yourself and your ability to sell. This is your belief system. You might tell me that you are motivated, focused, and have a history of closing the sales you want. Or, you might tell me you are lazy and rarely get what you want. Whatever you believe, you could point to the evidence in your life regarding why that is "true". If you believe you are inherently lazy and never get what you want, then you might have some beliefs surrounding how hard you have to work to make money. But if you believe that things usually come to you easily, and that's not happening at the moment, then you might have another block.

It is possible to be extremely motivated and focused on our businesses and not achieve our goals. How? Simple. There is something else blocking us. Most of the time it is self-created, and even more often, it is to protect us. I will go into more detail later regarding what stops most sales people from reaching their ultimate goals, but for right now,

> What you believe about selling directly correlates with your sales success.

just begin to tune into what you are saying to yourself on a conscious and subconscious level.

On the conscious level, you can quickly begin to discern exactly what you are saying to yourself if you just listen. Often we are saying a lot of negative things to ourselves about sales and sales people and we aren't even aware of it. For example, you might catch yourself saying things like...

- *Sales people are pushy...*

- *Money is dirty...*

- *People won't like me...*

- *Sales people are greedy...*

- *Selling is for used car salesmen...*

Once you begin to tune in, you might be really surprised about what you are saying to yourself. You might even realize that you have very negative beliefs about sales people and selling. Herein lies the secret: *What you believe about selling directly correlates with your sales success.* The good news is that you CAN change what you are saying to yourself as long as you become aware of it. Awareness always precedes change. Once you are aware, you can create a new script — new messages that you can begin to say to yourself and begin believing.

Subconscious beliefs are often more difficult to uncover because we can't "hear" them. However, it's very possible to "see" them by becoming aware of our behavior. For example, if you are deeply afraid of public speaking and avoid it at all costs, that is a behavior that you can observe. As you delve in deeper, ask yourself, *What does this behavior mean? Where did my fear of public speaking come from? What part of public speaking am I most afraid of?* You will begin to uncover a belief that you hold to be "true" about public speaking, and you may even be able to connect that belief with something that happened in your past. Whatever happened, it doesn't really matter. What matters is that once you are aware of that behavior, you can work toward changing it.

When I was in ninth grade, I developed a serious fear of public speaking. It was so serious that I wasn't even able

> Once you recognize your limiting beliefs about sales and selling, you can change them.

to read a paragraph in front of my classmates!

At a deeper level, what I really believed was that I wasn't good enough. What I had to change was my limiting belief about myself and recognize that I *was* good enough. I had two choices at that time: I could decide to let this fear take over and avoid public speaking at all costs, or I could decide to face it head on and overcome it. Thankfully, I chose the second option. During my sophomore year of high school, I enrolled in the Speech and Theater program. Let me tell you, this was not easy at all, but I knew that I needed to meet the fear head on if I was ever going to truly overcome it. Although I received quite a few red ribbons in the beginning, I went on to place in several competitions which inspired me to major in Communication in college. I received straight A's in my Communication courses in college, and my fear surrounding public speaking started to lessen.

Recently, one of my clients, the Vice President of Sales for a mid-size company, knew he was getting in his own way but just couldn't put his finger on why. We had coaching session after coaching session, and he just seemed to keep sabotaging his own efforts by not following through with the things he knew he needed to accomplish to sell more and to help his team sell more. Finally, we had a breakthrough session when I asked him to search deep down and figure out what was stopping him from reaching his sales goals. Out of nowhere he said, "I'm not good enough. I feel like a fraud, like people are going to find out that I'm really not good at what I do."

In fact, there were moments in his career when he had broken sales records and helped his team do the same. But then he would revert back to "status quo" and selling the bare minimum. By recognizing this negative belief and self-sabotaging behavior, he was able to create a new belief that helped him move forward in his business. That new belief was, *"I am enough."* By simply connecting with this new belief, he was able to move confidently in the direction of his own success. Last time I heard from him, he was planning on buying the company. As you can see, continuing to examine your own limiting beliefs and fears is critical to your sales success.

Once you recognize your limiting beliefs about sales and selling, you can change them. Changing a belief is as simple as changing a thought. At one time, maybe you believed that Santa Claus was real, and then you found out that he wasn't. All that changed was your thought. So now, think of a new thought that you would like to have about what selling means to you.

What would happen to your sales if you believed that...

- *Selling is easy?*
- *You solve your clients' problems?*
- *You coach your clients through their buying decisions?*
- *Your clients are grateful for your solutions?*
- *Your clients wonder where you've been all of their life?*
- *You are enough?*

Beliefs like these will transform the way you interact with your prospects and your clients, and it will transform your bottom line results.

Eleanor Roosevelt once said, "You must do the thing you think you cannot do." I did just that, and today, I am a paid professional speaker which has also made a positive impact on the sales revenue in my company. In a later chapter, we will examine how to overcome fear in greater detail, so begin to think about those fears that you are ready to take on, so you can reach your greatest sales goals!

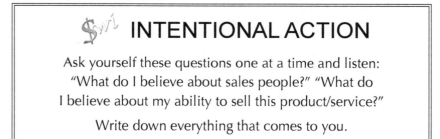

INTENTIONAL ACTION

Ask yourself these questions one at a time and listen:
"What do I believe about sales people?" "What do
I believe about my ability to sell this product/service?"

Write down everything that comes to you.

How Are You Doing?

Now that you know you already sell with intention, how would you rate yourself? On a scale of 1 to 10 (10 being the best), how are you doing? Are you selling with intention in a way that gets you more business or chases more prospects away? Perhaps you are saying things to yourself that are useless and demeaning and do not help you land more clients. If that's the case, congratulations! Now you must be wondering why I would congratulate you on giving yourself a low score in this area. Simple. All of us say negative things to ourselves (although I am sure there are some more enlightened individuals who can rise above this), so if you rated yourself a bit lower, that means that you are aware of what you are saying so that you can now change it!

If you didn't pick up on anything, it might be because it is either very deep in your subconscious, or you have not been in a quiet situation where you can connect with it.

💲 INTENTIONAL ACTION

Find a very quiet place where you will not be distracted.
Go back to the exercise on the previous page and try it again.
Let whatever is starting to surface in your mind just come forward. Whatever thoughts are there, just let them be there, and tune into the words.

You might be surprised at what you hear back from your very own mind. This might even be painful, but hang in there and listen to what you are saying. The words that you are hearing might be some of the most important words that you will hear in your life because they are your words; they are what you are saying to yourself, about yourself! You can't get much more powerful than that.

💲 INTENTIONAL ACTION

Whatever the words are, write them down.

By writing them down, you begin to take the power away from them, and now you can control them.

Look at the words you have written down.

What have you been saying to yourself about yourself?

Now, I must caution you, do not beat yourself up about the words that you are looking at. We can be our own worst enemies, but this is your chance to be your best friend.

> I want you to look down at those words and next to each one, write a new word. This new word should describe how you want to be as a sales person. Once you have written the new word, cross the old word out. It no longer serves you and you can give yourself permission to let go of the word and, more importantly, the power the word has had over you.
>
> Finally, look at those words one more time and the score you gave yourself. Then answer the following questions:
>
> What would it take for you to be at a level 10?
>
> What would be different in your sales career or business?
>
> In your life? Would your clients be different?

As you go through the rest of this book, keep that question in mind, and think about how you will know (what evidence will you have?) that you are at a level 10.

You might not be at a level 10 immediately, but you can begin to "act as if" in your inner and outer world. First, *see yourself at a level 10*, and then *present yourself as such to the world around you*. In other words, if you want to be an extremely successful sales person, make sure you look, act, and feel like one.

Positive and Intentional Affirmations

When you stop saying negative words to yourself, and begin saying positive affirmations, you will start to see positive changes first in yourself and then in your sales. I am sure we have all heard the importance of giving ourselves positive affirmations on a daily basis, but few people actually put that activity into practice. In order to make it a habit, it is extremely important to be intentional about how often we "feed" ourselves these positive words. I recommend that you

> You can let go of the power negative words have held over you.

have a set of positive affirmations that you can read to yourself three times per day if possible— more if you can! Simply saying "I am enough" can help you show up in a more confident way. Please note that powerful affirmations are most effective after you have released the limiting beliefs you can identify.

Equally important is examining the results you would like to achieve from saying these affirmations. For example, do you want to bring more clients into your life? Then you should have an affirmation that creates a feeling of deserving more clients, like "I am enough, and I help my clients easily solve their problems." Do you want to bring more money into your life? Then create an affirmation that draws more money into your life. One of my favorites that I frequently share with my clients is, "Money flows to me like a river!" Doesn't that just sound wonderful? Rivers typically have an unending flow of water, and that is exactly how I want money to flow to me, which is why I wrote the affirmation in that specific way. Again, the idea is to be very intentional about the affirmations you create for yourself (or borrow from others) in terms of the results you want to achieve by repeating them.

Memorizing your affirmations is great, but actually writing them down so you can refer back to them frequently is very important. Just the act of writing the affirmation down is more powerful to our brains than just trying to remember the words we were thinking about. You may want to write them on index cards and post the new, positive words in a place where you will see them — on your computer, your bathroom mirror, etc.

$wi **INTENTIONAL ACTION**

Create your set of Affirmation Cards. Read them three times daily.

The Final Word

You already sell with intention. Now it's your time to sell with intention in a way that serves you and the goals that you have in front of you. You can let go of the power that limiting beliefs have held over you by getting in touch with what you have been saying to yourself, choosing new words, and then repeating those words over and over to yourself daily. Awareness leads to change, and you are already on your way!

Remember, selling with intention means *you determine the result you want to achieve with a prospect before you even meet with them.*

TAKE A QUANTUM LEAP

For practical application — to really transform your thoughts and habits — visit www.SalesCoachNow.com and order your copy of our Selling With Intention workbook today.

For ongoing sales training and support, join our growing online community at www.MySalesCoachNow.com.

Know What You Want & How to Get It

"First, have a definite, clear practical ideal; a goal, an objective. Second, have the necessary means to achieve your ends; wisdom, money, materials, and methods.

Third, adjust all your means to that end."

— Aristotle —

What Do You Want?

*D*o you know what you want? Do you know how many clients you want this year? Prior to setting clear sales goals, you must gain clarity in what it is that you truly want to achieve in your sales career or business *and* your personal life. Without that level of clarity, you are not able to define your *Intentional Life Plan* and the goals that will help you manifest it. When you have clarity, you can then chunk each goal into smaller steps to ensure that you reach all of your goals and create your intentional life.

My second book *One Great Goal* was written to help people figure out what they really want in their personal and professional lives. Those of you who have completed that goal clarification process will find it easier to work through this chapter. If you haven't completed that process, the exercises in this section *will* help you begin to create an Intentional Life Plan; but if you find yourself feeling stuck or confused, consider picking up *One Great Goal* to gain clarity and connect your goals with your Soul Purpose.

Some of my clients know exactly what they want. Together, we create a plan that meets their needs, and then they go out into the world to make their daily, weekly, monthly and annual sales goals happen. They are excited, confident, and ready to make all of their goals happen so their Intentional Life Plan can manifest. And then sometimes, they will come back and say, "It didn't work. I wasn't able to close the deal with 'X' client." When I ask them, "What was your intention when you walked into the room to meet with your target client?" they might say, "Well, I wanted to develop the relationship so that we can do business together in the future." As their coach, I help them to see that they accomplished exactly what they intended and got what they wanted—maybe not on a conscious level, but on a subconscious level. They didn't intend to close the sale that day. Their intention was to develop a deeper relationship with their client, and they did just that. If you want to grow your sales, your intention must be clear and you need to know what you want.

What Do You Want for Your Personal Life?

By now you are probably saying, "Okay, so how do I even begin to figure out what I really want?" I'm sure you have had numerous conversations with yourself (in your mind) regarding all of the opportunities that are available to you. After all, we live in the United States of America where opportunities are abundant and waiting for those who know what they want!

The first step is to figure out what you want on a personal level: *Your life*. Hopefully, your business and sales goals have grown out of your personal goals. If they haven't, I would encourage you to think through your personal goals again and make sure you are clear on those first before you figure out your business goals. Answer these questions: *If I could create my life intentionally, what would it look like? And what would be one of the most important goals to achieve in order to manifest it?* For example, someone might say, "To manifest my intentional life, my goal is to be financially independent in five years and have enough excess money available to fund my non-profit and help foster youth."

Once you have defined your intentional life and determined some of your bigger goals, you need to be clear about the critical details of your life. Are you married? Single? What's your lifestyle like? Are you a spender? A saver? Do you want to take one vacation per year or twelve (I'm not joking!)? These are the kinds of questions you need to begin asking yourself so you can have a clear Intentional Life Plan that can then lead to a clear Intentional Sales Plan.

Before you create your Intentional Life Plan, make sure you have a clear picture of how you are spending your time right now. Is it balanced? Where do you need to make changes? How would you like to spend your time?

Many coaches today utilize a life balance wheel that typically includes the following areas: Health, Friendships, Personal Development, Finances, Family, Work/Career, Environments, Romantic Relationships, Recreation, Spiritual Life, etc. Usually, during the exercise, you shade in the "pie pieces" to illustrate how much time you are giving to specific areas in your life. Take out a piece of blank paper. Draw a large circle in the middle (it should take up most of the page). Then divide the circle into "pie slices" that illustrate how much time you spend in each area mentioned above.

I do believe that the life balance wheel is an excellent tool, and I would encourage you to use it. This simple exercise can help you see how much time you are spending in each area of your life and what you would like to change.

A clear Intentional Life Plan should also tell you how much your monthly expenses are, the amount of your annual travel for pleasure expenses, how much you want to save and invest each year, how much you donate, etc.

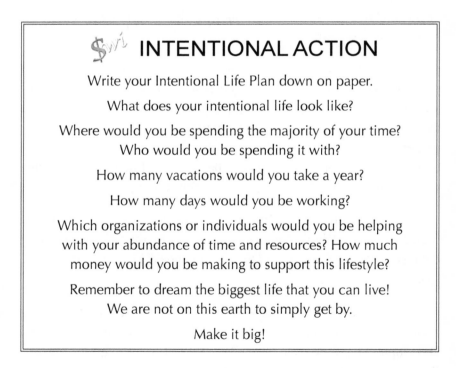

INTENTIONAL ACTION

Write your Intentional Life Plan down on paper.

What does your intentional life look like?

Where would you be spending the majority of your time?
Who would you be spending it with?

How many vacations would you take a year?

How many days would you be working?

Which organizations or individuals would you be helping with your abundance of time and resources? How much money would you be making to support this lifestyle?

Remember to dream the biggest life that you can live!
We are not on this earth to simply get by.

Make it big!

My Intentional Life

My Intentional Life Includes:

_____

_____

_____

_____

_____

_____

My Intentional Income:

Annual Income = "x" plus 25%: _____

OR

Annual Income = "x" times 2: _____

My intentional life affords me the following (Examples: flexible schedule, financial freedom, my dream house, charity contributions, etc.):

_____

_____

_____

_____

_____

My Intentional Life Achievement Date: _____

What is Your Intentional Sales Plan?

Now that you have an Intentional Life Plan that includes the goals that will help you to manifest it, it's time to create your Intentional Sales Plan. This should be in direct support of your life plan. Once you know what you want in life, it is so much easier to figure out what you want in your sales career or business.

In your Intentional Life Plan, you should have determined how much money your lifestyle demands that you make. Again, this is your intentional life, not just one that pays the bills. This dollar amount should be directly correlated with the financial goals in your business. Whatever the number is, I would encourage you to add 25% to it. Now, 25% is quite a bit, but I believe that everyone is living way under their level of potential, so adding 25% will help you think a little bigger. If you feel like you typically live under your potential, I want you to double the amount that you came up with. By getting out of the comfort zone that you have created, I guarantee that exciting things will begin to happen for you and your business!

- Intentional Life Annual Income = "X" + 25%
- OR, Intentional Life Annual Income = "X" * 2
- Intentional Life Affords me the Following:
  - Flexible Schedule
  - Extra Hours Every Day with My Family
  - A Second Home on the Beach
  - More Time for Recreational Activities
  - Financial Freedom

> Here's a secret that could be the most important secret revealed in this book:
>
> Make sure the goals are really what you want.

The new amount that you have calculated, adding either 25%, 100%, or more, is the number that you should work from. Your daily, weekly, monthly, and annual sales goals should grow out of this calculation. Calculate and figure out how many prospects you need to meet with on a daily basis to ensure that you reach your monthly goal. Thinking about your annual goal can be overwhelming, but when you break it down to daily steps and monthly goals, it suddenly becomes a whole lot more realistic. The exercises in this chapter will help you break it down into easy, can-do steps.

Are They Yours?

Now I am going to share a secret with you that could be the most important secret revealed in this book. It might sound simple to you once you read it, but I really want you to take the time to think about the significance of the words. Here goes: *Make sure the goals you have written down are really what you want!*

I know you are shaking your head right now, saying to yourself, "Well, of course it's what I want." But it might not be. Our minds are tricky. Sometimes we confuse what we want with what someone else wanted for us a long time ago. Check in on that. Is this goal something your dad wanted for you? Your mom? Your childhood teacher? If you realize that it's not *your* goal, that's okay. Just recognize and be aware of where the goal came from and go back and change it. And please know that it's okay. Better to be aware of it now than later! I was in my second semester of Law School before I realized that it wasn't even *my* goal.

> Give yourself permission to dream big and reach your goals.

Another question to ask is whether it truly is a *want* or a *need*. By answering this question, you can begin to discover more about the relationship you have with money. The relationship that you have with money and the beliefs you hold around your finances definitely control how you treat money today, but it doesn't have to be that way. Answer this simple question, and to make sure the question is effective, answer with the first word that comes to your mind.

Is having more money a *want* or a *need*?

If you answer that it is a *want*, you are well on your way to financial success because in your mind you know it is okay to want more money so you can live the kind of life you want to live. Having more money also means that you can engage in the philanthropic endeavors you are passionate about. If you said that it is a *need*, you might still be living paycheck to paycheck or well below your capability. In that case, you might want to further investigate your limiting beliefs about money. One of my favorite books that I found really helpful in this area is T. Harv Eker's *Secrets of the Millionaire Mind*.

A-GAIN: Our 5-Step Process for Making It a Reality

Now that you are really clear about what you want, how can you make it happen? At *Sales Coach Now*, we have developed a simple, five-step process (A-GAIN: **A**ssessment, **G**ap-Analysis and Goal-Setting, **A**ccountability, **I**ntentional and Inspired Action, and **N**ever, Never, Never Give Up!) for goal achievement that can be applied to any goal.

Step #1 - Assessment

How are you doing? Are you closing enough sales? Do you find that you are under pressure at the end of every month because you haven't reached your sales goal? Assessment means that you take the time to understand your current sales results and what might be causing pain in your business. Ask yourself, *What is my sales goal? Am I on track to reach it? And by what date do those sales need to be closed?*

What is not reaching your sales goals costing you personally and in your business/career? How could reaching your sales goals impact your business and life in a positive manner?

_____

_____

_____

_____

_____

On a scale of 1-10 (1 will be low, 10 will be high), rate your current satisfaction with your sales results. Based on the number you choose, please explain what it would take for you to feel like it's a "10".

_____

_____

_____

_____

_____

What will reaching your sales goals make possible for you that is even MORE important?

1. _____

2. _____

3. _____

4. _____

5. _____

6. _____

7. _____

When do you want to reach your sales goal every month?

_____

_____

For those of you who know what you want (*As I mentioned, you may benefit from reading my second book* One Great Goal *and going deeper into the process.*), you must ask yourself, *How can I make sure it happens by this certain date?* Creating your Intentional Life Plan and Intentional Sales Plan is a great first step. From there, it's important to review the goals you have determined will help you create your intentional personal and professional life on a quarterly basis. Reviewing monthly can sometimes be too much because you might not have given your goals enough time to happen. Reviewing on a quarterly basis gives you the evidence and results from three months, which should give you a pretty clear picture of how you are doing. Remember to ask for this sales goal or something better.

A great way to assess your sales progress is to put your sales projections and results into an excel spreadsheet. On a daily, weekly, and monthly basis, you will be able to intentionally measure your results.

If It Doesn't Feel Good Anymore, Let It Go

Upon reviewing your goals quarterly, you might discover that the goals you were originally so sure of are no longer what you want. If you realize that, congratulations because you have just saved yourself a whole lot of time and energy! The key is to give yourself permission to change your mind and create new goals that better support your overall dream. And please, let yourself off the hook! There are too many over-achievers out there who refuse to let go of goals that no longer serve them because they are afraid of feeling like a failure. Failing is really about not doing what's right for you rather than not achieving your goals. If you need help in this area, speak with a trusted mentor or friend. Explain to them that you are having a hard time giving yourself permission to let go of a goal. Ask them if they have ever changed their mind about the achievement of a goal. Find out how they let themselves off the hook.

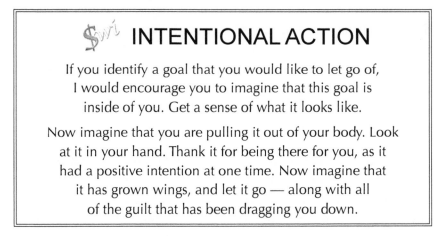

INTENTIONAL ACTION

If you identify a goal that you would like to let go of, I would encourage you to imagine that this goal is inside of you. Get a sense of what it looks like.

Now imagine that you are pulling it out of your body. Look at it in your hand. Thank it for being there for you, as it had a positive intention at one time. Now imagine that it has grown wings, and let it go — along with all of the guilt that has been dragging you down.

For some people, even realizing that a goal is not right might be difficult. There are many of us walking the planet simply not in touch with our internal world. We like to believe that we are, but the reality is that we are not. If you fall into this category, it is important for you to begin to get in touch with your "gut" instinct. A gut instinct is the intuitive side of your being that can help you change directions and make better decisions if you are able to tune into it. I have heard people say, "Yes, but I am just not intuitive." I'm sorry, but that excuse doesn't work!

Sometimes a gut feeling can come through in the form of feeling physically ill when you are in a specific situation or around a specific person. Every time you have this experience, you feel ill (but please do not confuse this with a phobia that requires professional help). For example, you might feel physically ill whenever you attend a specific networking group but not another. Why? Your body might be trying to tell you that the first group is just not a good fit for you, your business, or the achievement of your goals. Pay attention! You might be wasting a whole lot of energy in a group that does not serve your overall goals. Trust your gut instinct. It's usually right!

Step #2 - Gap Analysis and Goal-Setting

Now that you have set your goal — including your intentional life, annual income, and the achievement date — you must look at the steps you will need to take to reach it. This is the gap in between. Understanding the steps in the gap is key to ensuring that you will reach your goals. Once you identify the steps that you have to take to reach your goal, it is then important to break them down into even smaller, achievable steps.

Turn those achievable steps into clear and realistic action items designed to help you reach your sales goals. If you read one of your action items and it is actually more than one step, you need to break it down even further. Each step should feel simple and clear, or it needs more attention. Also, make sure that each step has a completion date attached to it. Please note that sometimes you are only aware of the next step, not the next ten. Just take the next step that you see.

Write Every Step Down

The trainers at the NLP Institute of California stressed the importance of setting goals and intentions on a daily, weekly, and monthly basis. Think how different your business would be if every day you knew exactly the outcome that you expected. For example, let's say that you expected to see five prospects one day and turn three of those five into clients that same day. Wow! That would be a great day, particularly if the other two turned into clients in the near future. What would happen if you wrote that goal in your day timer? Would it suddenly seem more real to you? How much greater do you think your odds would be of achieving that goal?

Statistics say that the odds of achieving goals are much greater if you write them down. In an excerpt from *What They Don't Teach You at Harvard Business School* by Mark McCormack, he discusses a study that was conducted with the 1979 graduates of the Harvard MBA program. They were asked if they had clear, written goals for the future and whether or not they had plans to accomplish them.

- Only 3% had written goals and plans
- 13% had goals but not in writing
- 84% had no specific goals

Ten years later, in 1989, the students were interviewed again. The 13% who had their goals in memory were earning twice as much as the 84% who had no specific goals. The 3% who had clear written goals ten years earlier were earning ten times as much as the other 97% of graduates all together. So, again, how much greater would the odds be of achieving your goals if you wrote them down in your day timer?

Many people finally figure out what they want but never take that next step of writing it down.

My Target Client Goals

Number of Clients in the Previous Year: _____

Number of Clients I Want This Year (based upon annual income goals above):_____

The Difference: _____ _____

Completion Date to Have Those New Clients:_____

Or

Monthly Client Goal (if you must attract new clients every month):

How Did I Get There?

A Visualization Exercise

Close your eyes and imagine that you have reached your target client goal. Turn in a half circle and face the opposite direction. Imagine that there is a timeline in front of you between where you are standing (your completion date) all the way back to today's date. Look at the timeline and imagine that the steps you took to reach your goal are clearly laid out before you. Look at them. Remember them. Then, look at the timeline and notice what you had to let go of to reach your goals. What do you see?

Action Plan! Put your VISION into ACTION! During the visualization, what steps did you need to take in your business to reach your goals?

1. _____

2. _____

3. _____

4. _____

5. _____

Now, prioritize those steps!

1. _____

2. _____

3. _____

4. _____

5. _____

Put your goals into action. Write down each goal and the date that you will complete it.

1. _____

2. _____

3. _____

4. _____

5. _____

What Do I Need to Let Go Of?

Refer back to your Visualization Exercise when you imagined the timeline. What did you notice that you needed to let go of in order to reach your goal?

For example, you might need to let go of limiting beliefs that are getting in your way, old goals or ways of doing things, etc.

1. _____

2. _____

3. _____

4. _____

5. _____

You have now created an Intentional Life Plan and an Intentional Sales Plan, and you understand the importance of writing it down. Now take a look at that plan. Take time to carefully go through it and break down each goal into smaller steps. Once you have gone through this process and broken each goal into manageable steps, go through the smaller steps and see if they need to be broken down even more. If you are already aware of one or two steps, that's fine; just take that next step and see what unfolds from there.

For example, one of your goals might be to close 10 sales per month. This is a wonderful, worthy goal, but how will you do it? First, you need to know what your closing ratio is. For ease of numbers, let's say it's 50%. That means you need to meet with 20 prospects to close 10 sales. Assuming that your ratio for getting appointments is also 50%, your smaller goal would then be to contact 40 prospects to set up those 20 appointments. As you can see, each goal will have numerous steps underneath it that will be necessary to reach the overall goal. Take the time to break each goal down so that you can accomplish it with ease.

The Intentional Life and Sales Plans will be very thorough to ensure that you can reach your goals by…when? It is critical that you have a date set next to each major goal as well as every baby step. Without a timeline for achievement, you may never reach any of your goals! I know this sounds harsh but, unfortunately, I have seen this happen over and over and have felt awful for those individuals. A goal without a date is like being at the shooting range without a target to aim for. You will simply be shooting blind and may never end up where you set your sights. I do not want that to happen to you, so please be clear on your achievement dates. Finally, adding dates to your scheduled rewards is incredibly exciting as well and, from a behavioral standpoint, will help you turn this behavior into a habit!

Step #3 - Accountability

Now that you have the steps broken down, it is time to take action. Keep a list of your action items with you at all times to keep you motivated and cross them off as you complete them. Then find a trusted mentor, coach, business associate or someone else to hold you accountable to reaching your goals. Meet with them as often as you can to discuss your progress or the challenges you might be facing.

Ask for Support

Tell others about your Intentional Life and Sales Plans and the steps you have created to achieve them. When you tell someone, you are suddenly not the only one invested in your goal. Having someone who now supports you on your journey can be incredibly powerful. Just be selective when you choose someone — make sure they really do care about your best interest.

Telling someone also gives you a level of accountability that you would not otherwise have on your own. You may want to create your very own support team. This support team could include mentors, business associates and friends. Having a variety of perspectives will ensure that you can talk through your dream at any time and get the best feedback possible. The advice will vary, so it will be up to you to sort through it and pull out the information that is the most valuable to you. One person in that group might be a good fit for what I like to refer to as an accountability partner. This is someone who supports you and your Intentional Life Plan and, in return, you support his or her Intentional Life Plan.

Who are five people I can ask to hold me accountable to my goals?

1. _____

2. _____

3. _____

4. _____

5. _____

Step #4 - Intentional and Inspired Action

After you have set your goals, pay attention to the ideas that suddenly show up — especially those ideas that feel intentional and inspired! The difference between really successful sales people who have made it and those who haven't is *inspired action*. When they have a hunch or gut instinct, they follow it. And when a door swings wide open, they don't question it, but rather walk straight through and then decide what to do next.

For a long time, I had this "idea" of creating a virtual sales training and coaching community. However, for two years it was just that — an "idea". There were many times when I could have acted on the idea, but I kept pushing it out of my mind because it felt like "too much" to take on due to everything else that was on my plate. Have you ever felt like that? As more and more non-productive activities came off my plate, I suddenly noticed that I had more space in my brain to think about and consider moving forward with this inspired idea. And then one day, I just decided that it was time to take real action!

After doing research for a week, we discovered the perfect company to assist us with getting the community off the ground. The name also came to me "out of nowhere" —*Sales Coach Now* — but I knew that it was another inspired idea that had come through because I was listening. I know that when we make the "mind space", the ideas flow. From there, I set a thirty day launch date. Yes, I announced to clients, colleagues, friends, and family that we would launch *Sales Coach Now* at a live event in thirty days. Wow! The pressure was on!

Having set the date, the inspirational ideas and actions that I needed to take came pouring into my mind with ease. Although I worked long days to keep moving forward, I stayed tuned in and listened for the next step. Less than thirty days later, we launched *Sales Coach Now* with a live audience of one hundred guests. That night we were blessed to sell enough *Sales Coach Now* memberships to ensure that in the first month, it was a profitable venture! When I look back, I know it happened because I was faithful in listening for the next step I needed to take.

Step #5 - Never, never, never give up!

In the words of Winston Churchill, never give up! Stay on your path to sales success no matter what obstacles you might be facing! That is exactly what the "N" in "A-GAIN" stands for.

There are going to be times when you feel like giving up. You may realize that you are feeling fearful or doubtful or discouraged. When you notice that feeling, you have a choice to make: You can either decide to give up, or you can acknowledge the feeling and keep moving toward your goal anyway. My advice? Keep moving anyway.

Tying It All Together

Think about how you will ensure your success. Part of reaching your goals after you have set the action items into motion is having faith and trusting that with the right action, it will happen.

What do you want to make sure that you remember from this experience in order to remain motivated on your journey?

What are five ways this plan will impact my sales?

1. _____

2. _____

3. _____

4. _____

5. _____

Keeping Your Plan in Motion With Intention

Once the plan is in motion, it is crucial to keep it in motion. The best way to do this is by making a daily habit of setting clear intentions for your personal life and your business.

- *What would it be like if you set your intention before you started your day?*
- *Before every networking meeting?*
- *Before every prospect meeting?*

You get the idea. Having a clear intention can make your job so much easier because people will sense that you mean business, and you will be focused in a way that will allow you to reach your goals.

First, make sure that you are clear internally about your intention. When I work with clients, I will often ask them what their intention is in a specific situation. Is it to get to know the prospect better? Or is it to close a deal and move forward? You'd be surprised how many people go in with the first intention, but really wanted to come out with the second. Choose the intention that you really want.

Now some of you might be saying, "That sounds too easy. It will never work." For the sales veterans out there, this is what they do every day. They set their intention and then they assume the sale. Assuming the sale means that their intention is to do business with this prospect, and they will find a way to make that happen. Their attitude is, "Whatever it takes." They do not plan on coming back again and again. Their goal is to shorten the sales cycle because their time is extremely valuable and they are confident they can solve their client's problem. And when they meet with their prospects, it shows. Would you rather buy from someone who is confident they can solve your problem or someone who just wants to get to know you better?

You have a plan, you know you want it, and you will do whatever it takes to make it happen. Now, you must see it actually happening! Visualizing success is a tool that most people do not take advantage of on a regular basis. Now take a moment to visualize your entire year of success using the following visualization exercise.

INTENTIONAL ACTION:
VISUALIZATION EXERCISE

Close your eyes.

Imagine stepping into the future one years from now (or whatever the date is), having already achieved your sales goal.

Standing in your date of achievement, imagine that there is a timeline in front of you that stretches all the way back to today's date.

Look at your personal and business plans and see yourself achieving each goal on your timeline like a movie playing out in your mind.

Now, start the movie over and this time make the colors ten times brighter. Grow it so it is the size of an Imax Theater Screen. Add sound. What do you hear? What do you smell? Tune into all of your senses! How do you feel inside? However you are feeling, make that feeling even larger. Breathe into it!

Finally, with all of your senses cued up, watch your success story of the year one more time, and see yourself creating your intentional life!

TAKE A QUANTUM LEAP

For practical application — to really transform your thoughts and habits — visit www.SalesCoachNow.com and order your copy of our Selling With Intention workbook today.

For ongoing sales training and support, join our growing online community at www.MySalesCoachNow.com.

Be the Problem-Solver

"When the mind is thinking, it is talking to itself."

— Plato —

Sales and Psychology

*E*very successful sales person I know does one thing well: They understand the impact of psychology on the sale. The marketing industry is filled with experts in psychology who have helped their clients achieve great results by applying psychology to their marketing efforts. However, the same cannot be said for sales. In my experience, most sales people either "get it" and understand the impact of psychology on sales, or they don't. If you do, you are one of the lucky few, and feel free to skip this chapter (or not!). If you don't have that level of understanding, please read on, so I can give you a few secrets regarding the psychology of the sale (my graduate degree in psychology really paid off!).

Psychology is about understanding people and their behavior. In other words, *"What makes people do what they do?"* What *influences* people to behave the way they do? Psychology is defined as *"the science of the mind and human behavior"* according to the *American Heritage Dictionary.*

For the purposes of this book, psychology is the study of why people act or behave in certain ways when presented with different opportunities. If you can understand why people do what they do, you can significantly increase your chances of closing a sale.

Pleasure, Pain & The Problem You Solve

Human beings are *pleasure seekers* and *pain avoiders.* Think about that for a minute. Yes, that is boiling human behavior down to a very basic level, but at a basic level, that is how humans make most of their decisions. If you can keep that simple fact in mind when you are selling, you will become more aware of your clients' decision-making process.

At one time in history, many thousands of years ago, being a pleasure seeker and a pain avoider was the key to survival. Eating was a pleasure (and critical to survival), and avoiding pain meant running from wild animals that could kill you. This is survival at the most basic level. I hope you are laughing at this point because my goal is to make this concept so simple it burns into your brain so you can retrieve this bit of information whenever you need it!

Today, your clients and prospects live in a world that still involves survival at a basic level whether or not they consciously think about it (believe me, your subconscious thinks about it all the time!). For example, most people love to eat (pleasure seeking) and we also try to avoid pain at all costs (avoiding cold-calling!). However, in this day and age, most of us are no longer hunters and gatherers. Instead, we are now living in an information age that still involves high levels of stress and fear every day that can make pleasure seeking and pain avoiding an even bigger issue for people.

So, you are probably asking, "What does this all mean to me — the sales person or business owner?" Your clients and prospects are human, so that means that they are pleasure seekers and pain avoiders at the most basic level. Got it? You need to sell to those basic levels. To do that, you need to figure out what their problems are.

Now, this is not to be unethical or unprofessional. Rather, this is your opportunity to understand what might fuel their desire to purchase your product or service. For example, if you are selling a high tech IT solution, you must determine the problem that you solve and the pain you help them avoid. I would guess that it is because your high tech IT solution solves productivity problems and the pain of downtime.

Are you getting this? If your solution can deliver results that solve their problem and help them avoid pain, then they can do the things they enjoy (like spend time with family). And you have just satisfied their two basic needs to increase their pleasure and avoid pain.

 INTENTIONAL ACTION:
VISUALIZATION EXERCISE
Close your eyes, and visualize your Top 2 Prospects at
this very moment. Really get a sense of who they are, their
personalities, and how they may try to avoid pain.
What do you see? What are their challenges?
What problem does your product/service solve for them?

Your "Problem-Solving" Message

When I worked in the IT Industry, we helped clients satisfy their IT training needs so they could reach their technology goals on an ongoing and timely basis. If they didn't get their IT team trained in a timely manner, they would have major pain and problems because the technology they depended upon would not be running correctly. Or, their end-users would have no idea what to do because their technology managers didn't receive the

> Human beings are pleasure seekers and pain avoiders. If you keep that in mind when you are selling, you will begin to see the impact in your sales.

proper knowledge to pass on. The IT training sales people had to understand what the cost would be to the company if the proper training didn't happen in the right timeframe. Once they understood that, they could really support the customer, solve their problems, and help them with their overall goals.

A "problem-solving" message summarizes the problem you solve and the pain you help your clients avoid. Do you have a "problem-solving" message, or is your message focused on only the benefits of your product or service? If it's just focused on the benefits, you might be missing out on sales.

Some prospects will buy simply based on pleasure or because your product or service improves their situation. For others, however, they really need to hear how you can solve a real problem — a real pain — that they are experiencing. If you are in the service business, the service you offer will, I guarantee, solve a problem that your prospect is having. You might be in the house-cleaning business. For a working family, it can be an annoying problem to come home and have to clean an entire house. By offering your service, you are able to take the pain and exhaustion of cleaning from working parents. Any working family out there will tell you that a service like that is worth its weight in gold! Products also solve very specific problems. What problem does your service or product solve?

Once you understand the problem that your product or service solves, you can then create a "problem-solving" message. The "problem-solving" message should be one sentence that explains who your clients are, the problem that you solve, and the results your clients will achieve. For example, *I specialize in helping entrepreneurs and sales professionals take the pain out of selling so that they can effortlessly grow their sales.* Wow! That's powerful, and having more sales would certainly take a lot of pain away from many organizations. Plus, do you see how easy it is for me to talk about what I do through that one sentence? Write your own "problem-solving" message now!

> Once you know where you stand with your clients, you can become better at delivering your solution and know you are actually solving their problems.

The Importance of Delivering Quality

Once the prospect has chosen you as their provider of choice, it is up to you to deliver a quality product without pain! This sounds simple. We should all be able to deliver our products and services in a timely fashion, but let me tell you, it does not always happen that way. I have seen businesses fail to deliver on their promises, and I am sure you have experienced this yourself. If you are telling your target prospects that your product or service will solve their problem, and in the end it causes even more, then you are simply not doing your job, or the company you work for has some internal challenges. Even taking an extra day or hour to deliver your services might be too much for some clients. If you want quality target prospects to hire you, then you need to make sure that you are offering quality products and services that deliver whatever you promise. If you can do that, you will gain clients for life.

Let's imagine now that you are going to deliver your products and services in a timely fashion, and deliver the quality products and services that you've committed to. When you successfully solve your clients' problems, I can almost guarantee that they will want more of what you have delivered and continue to be a client. Over time, you will actually begin to condition your client to want more of what you offer. This idea belongs to early American Psychologist and Harvard Professor B.F. Skinner, one of the masters in the field of human behavior who applied scientific methods to the idea of conditioning.

Once your clients are really enjoying your products and services, becoming conditioned to want more, something exciting will start to happen. What, you ask? Well, my friend, your clients will begin telling their friends and other people they know how much your products or services help them. Wow! And then, you will begin to receive referrals!

Now, people might not always think about offering referrals to you, so sometimes you have to ask. Do not be afraid to ask, even if they say no. Most people like to help others, so their natural inclination will be to say, "Yes, I know so and so," and generously give you the information you desire. One word of caution: In my humble opinion, I suggest that you ask for referrals in a very professional manner so as not to offend. You want to retain your client for life, and not make them feel like they're being taken advantage of.

What Do Your Clients Say?

On that note, how can you truly measure how your clients feel about you? I have worked with many people who want to ask for referrals, but they don't because of their fear of rejection. It is very important to know how your clients feel about you so that you can be confident that you are delivering the best possible service or products to them. Now, some people just know because they hear it over and over from their clients and prospects. The reality is that if 99% of your clients are telling you that the solution you have delivered is outstanding, believe them and capitalize on your success!

If, however, none of your clients have ever said that to you, begin to ask yourself some hard questions. And, in order to improve, you must be honest with yourself: *Am I delivering top quality products and services consistently?* If you get an immediate *yes*, yet you are one of those people who have never heard it from their customers, I would encourage you to take this one step further and actually ask your clients. Yes, ask them!

Now, I would recommend that you get a third party to help you with a survey so that it does not feel threatening to your clients. Basically, you can send out an anonymous survey to find out how you can become better as a business or sales professional. The document, however, will ask questions regarding what clients like or don't like about your products or services. Be prepared for honest feedback if you ask for it. Once you know where you stand with your clients, you can become better at solving their problems.

After surveying their clients to see how they are doing, some people find out that they are way off-base in terms of what their clients actually want. What your client wants is the answer to the question we posed earlier which was, "What is causing you pain in your business right now?" If our businesses are to be successful, we must give clients what they want, not what we think they need.

In addition to surveying all of your existing clients, I would encourage you to make sure that you are always doing a thorough "WANTS" analysis (as opposed to a "NEEDS" analysis). We can tell clients all day long what we think they need, but if we truly figure out what they want (they want you to solve their problem), our products or services will make a much more dramatic impact on their business. A "WANTS" analysis stands for:

Wants

A

New

Terrific

Solution

="NEEDS", on the other hand, stands for:

Not

Even

Encompassing

the

Desired

Solution

Now many of us (including myself) have been taught to do a "NEEDS" analysis, so it will be difficult to take on this new way of thinking. However, I have found that when I focus on a "WANTS" analysis, I find terrific solutions that are customized to make a real difference for the client and truly solve their problem. Even if you sell a product, how you deliver that product could be customized specifically for your client or prospect. When we focus on giving clients what they truly want, and solve their problems, we will have clients for life!

$₩ℓ **INTENTIONAL ACTION**

Make a list of the problems that you solve for your clients. Then, create your problem-solving message!

TAKE A QUANTUM LEAP

For practical application — to really transform your thoughts and habits — visit www.SalesCoachNow.com and order your copy of our Selling With Intention workbook today.

For ongoing sales training and support, join our growing online community at www.MySalesCoachNow.com.

Define Your Target Client

"To my customer: I may not have the answer, but I'll find it. I may not have the time, but I'll make it. I may not be the biggest, but I'll be the most committed to your success."

— Author Unknown —

Your Target Client

Who is your target client? At first glance, this sounds like an easy question. It is a question that I ask during our *Selling With Intention* Intensive Courses. Time is spent just getting a clear picture of who it is that you want to work with. And the next question I ask is, "What if all of your prospects were target clients?" This gets many participants grinning from ear-to-ear across the room. Inevitably, a line forms across their forehead as the doubt creeps in: "Is that even possible? Is it possible to have a business where I work only with target clients?" Anything is possible when you are clear about what you want and intentional about getting it, and when you believe that there are enough clients for everyone.

The first step in gaining clarity about who your target clients are is to get clear on who you do not want to work with. Yes, I am suggesting that there are prospects that are not a good fit for you or your business, and are not worth pursuing. That does not mean that they are bad people or bad companies. It simply means that there is another company out there that will be a better fit for them.

Some indications that a prospect might not be a target client for your business include you feeling ill whenever you meet with them, call them, or have to return an e-mail. You might be laughing right now because you are saying, "Yes, I have prospects and clients like that!" Clients or prospects that leave you feeling drained and unmotivated will not help you reach your ultimate goals. Typically, they have a host of other issues going on that you might not be qualified to help with, but you can certainly refer others who might be able to help. The reality is that you may never make these clients happy — ever! — and they will never refer you business. In the end, the relationship could end poorly, which could inadvertently damage your reputation. Getting clear on who you do not want to work with will save you a lot of pain in the long run!

When I first started my own business, I didn't know that I could be "picky" about the clients I worked with. In the beginning, I felt like I just needed to pay my bills. About four months after launching my business, I received a referral from someone I had just met, and she told me that the prospect had a sales team that needed some help. I met with the owner later that week. The meeting went well, but I had a nagging feeling in my stomach that something wasn't quite right. Instead of listening to my intuition, I worked hard to close that sale anyway. Six months later, I was miserable and questioning everything about my business. The contract finally came to an end, and as I drove out of their parking lot, I told myself that I would never again work with a client that wasn't a good fit.

Non-Target Clients

For those of you who provide a service to your clients, letting go of those who do not fit will probably be even more difficult. Usually, if you are in a service business, you have a natural inclination to help others. That can get you into all kinds of difficult situations because your desire to help might sometimes be greater than your ability to discern between those you can help and those who think they want to be helped.

If you find yourself attracting a lot of clients who seem impossible to help, I would really advise you to check in on what this means about you. Now, I am not criticizing anyone here, but having a healthy understanding of what is underneath your desire to help others is pretty important if you are going to appeal to the kind of clients that you desire to attract.

Most of the time, we attract clients who are exactly where we are in our lives and businesses right now. So, if you want to attract clients who are successful

> The first step in gaining clarity about your target clients is to get clear on who you do NOT want to work with.

and at the top of their game, that's where you need to be too. If you are attracting clients who are depressed and unmotivated (if you are a therapist, this might be very different for you), check in on how you are feeling. Typically, if you are feeling confident and on top of the world, then people who are confident and on top of the world will be drawn to you. So, take care of your own personal development first, so that you can attract the kind of clients you desire.

The Price of Non-Target Clients

First, you have to know that it is okay for you to say *no* to prospects if it is simply not a good fit. Ethically, this is really important. Whether you are selling a product or a service, you still have the responsibility to be honest with the prospect rather than just take their money.

The second point to recognize is that targeting prospects that are not the right fit is just a bad use of your time. Do not, and I mean do not, waste your time selling to prospects who you know are not right for you or your business or because you need the money. It may be in your comfort zone to sell to people that you see as "safe". However, if you can get out of your comfort zone and have the courage to sell to someone you know will truly benefit from your services and is the absolute right fit, then it is your duty to give them the opportunity to buy.

Stacy Hall and Jan Brogniez, in their book *Attracting Perfect Customers*, teach their readers how to attract perfect customers into their business on a consistent basis. They talk about developing "Strategic Synchronicity" in your business to make attracting perfect customers seamless. Hall and Brogniez write,

> As we have explored previously, the way to recognize a perfect customer is to first design a prototype of what your perfect customers would look like: How they would behave, what qualities and talent they would possess, what products and services they would purchase from you, what amount of money they would pay you, and how often they would need or purchase your products or services or visit your web site.

I highly recommend this book to help you delve even deeper to find out exactly who the best clients are for your business.

You will know if you aren't working with your target clients because you will begin to dislike what you do! That's the first indication. You will probably notice that getting out of bed in the morning is no longer something you look forward to. When you think of that client, you will probably get a pain in your stomach or feel sick in some way. And the longer you work with that client, the worse things will get. (I am speaking from experience!)

Soon, you will probably begin to take it out on your spouse or your family. Some of you are nodding your head "Yes!" right now because you remember, maybe even

> If you can get in touch with who you are at a deep, core level, you will more easily attract target clients and success into your business and life.

recently, taking something out on your spouse because you were dissatisfied at work. If it goes on even longer, you will begin to question why you are even in your particular industry. I'm not kidding. I had a client who told me that one of his clients had made him so "angry" that he had even begun to question why he had ever gotten into the business he was in! He was ready to throw in the towel when I said to him, "You have to let go of this client so you can move on. Once you do that, you will be able to clearly evaluate whether or not you truly want to leave." He let go of the client, moved on, and began attracting and working only with his target clients. He loves his business again.

The Best Clients for You

Finding your target clients is not about going out and looking for them. Instead, you need to get really clear on who the best clients are for your product or service, and then you can more easily figure out where they are. One way to get clear on who you want to work with is to understand who you are.

Yes, you read that correctly: *Figure out who you are*. I recognize that this can be a life-long process, so just stick with who you are right now at this moment. After all, that's who your clients will be dealing with. To simplify, we need only refer to The Law of Attraction: *Like attracts like*. We like to work with people who are like us. Simple, right? It is easier to attract your target clients once you are clear on who you are. Now, let me clarify that I am not talking about your race, ethnicity, sexual orientation, etc. I *am*, however, talking about your likes, dislikes, beliefs, values, etc.

Who are you? This question by itself can raise fear. After all, life can be a search to find out who we really are, and it seems to be a moving target as we change over time. Yet, we all know people who really, truly know themselves at a deep core level. We want to identify with them because they seem to attract success and opportunities effortlessly. Their personalities are magnetic and they draw their target clients to them easily — like a magnet. If you can get in touch with who you are at a deep, core level, you too will more easily attract target clients and success into your business and life.

 ## INTENTIONAL ACTION:
—WHO YOU ARE—PART I

Make a list of the top fifteen qualities that you like about yourself. Sometimes we are so disconnected with who we are that we say things like, "I am President of ABC Company," or "I am the owner of five successful businesses." That is not who you are, that is what you do or have done. Somehow as a society we have confused who we are with what we do. If you aren't what you do, then who are you?

INTENTIONAL ACTION:
—WHO YOU ARE—PART II

I want you to think back to when you were seven years old. Get a visual of yourself. An image. Then, step into that little person.

> What do you feel? Where are you? At seven years old, we are
> dreamers and believers. We believe that anything is possible
> and we know that we can make all of our dreams come true.
> Typically, we are most in touch with our true selves at that age.
> What are your likes and dislikes as you step into this little person?
> Values? Morals? Write them down. Now you are beginning to get
> a picture of who you really are at a core level.
>
> Some of these parts might have been lost, but you can easily bring
> them back to you now. Once you are in touch with your true self,
> it will be much easier to attract your target clients to you.

Another way to get in touch with who you are is to tune in to where you like to spend your time. Think about a time and place where you have felt incredibly alive and excited about your life and your business (yes, both together).

- Where are you?

- What are you doing?

- Who is it that surrounds you? *Perhaps you are at a special networking meeting where you really enjoy the people who attend. Or maybe you are at church or another non-profit organization that really makes you feel alive.*

- See yourself connecting with the people around you. *Notice how those people who are attracted* to you seem to almost "vibrate" at the same energy level.

Now, when it happens naturally, it is usually because you are speaking to someone like yourself, and the attraction process just unfolds naturally as you easily build rapport with them. Sound simple? That's because it is! Spend time at the professional organizations you really enjoy, and it is likely that your prospects and referral partners will be there too.

Your Favorite Client

One easy way to take this a step further is to think of one client that you have right now who is your utmost favorite. For example, you always enjoy working with them or seeing them, and when you leave a meeting with them, you feel energized and excited about your business. Your favorite client probably also values your products or services, your time, who you are, etc. Whatever it is, there are some clear reasons why you believe this person is your favorite client. Create a list of all of their qualities and the reasons that you enjoy working with them so you can begin to get clear on who your target clients might be.

What are the top 15 qualities of your favorite client?

1. _____

2. _____

3. _____

4. _____

5. _____

6. _____

7. _____

8. _____

9. _____

10. _____

11. _____

12. _____

13. _____

14. _____

15. _____

Finish this sentence: "My favorite client always wants me to..."

1. _____

2. _____

3. _____

4. _____

5. _____

6. _____

7. _____

8. _____

9. _____

10. _____

INTENTIONAL ACTION:
VISUALIZATION EXERCISE

I want you to get in touch with as many of your senses as possible as you imagine your encounter with your favorite client. Think back to the last transaction or deal that you finished with them.

Remember how you felt in that moment while you were with them. Let that feeling, whatever it is, grow even bigger! Perhaps you were excited, motivated or just plain happy.

Let the visual that you have created grow even larger so that it encompasses your entire picture, almost like an Imax screen in front of you. Add color and then take that color and make it ten times as bright. Can you see it?

What do you see? Zoom in on your face and take a look at your expression. Amazing! Look at your body language.

How are you communicating non-verbally? What do you look like when you are with your favorite client?

Now, multiply whatever feelings you are having inside by ten as well. Wow! What is that like?

Finally, get in touch with what you are smelling and hearing around you and allow those senses to become even sharper.

Got it?

What would your business be like if every day felt like this? I bet it would be amazing!

Now that you have visualized your favorite client, I want you to check in on what it is they appreciate about you.

INTENTIONAL ACTION: VISUALIZATION EXERCISE

Imagine that you and your favorite client have just sat down at your favorite coffee shop to enjoy your favorite beverage. You have a legal pad and a pen in front of you.

Look across the table at your favorite client.

(Again, this is a visualization exercise, although you could also do it in person if you have an excellent relationship and your client is open to this kind of conversation.)

Now ask the following question: "What do you appreciate about me in terms of our business relationship?"

If you allow yourself to have this visualization, just begin to write down whatever you imagine they would say. This is really an exercise in free-writing because ideas and thoughts will come to you quickly when you ask this question.

Don't miss a word! Write for as long as you can.

Five minutes would be ideal — or at least thirty items.

What does your favorite client appreciate about you?

1. _____

2. _____

3. _____

4. _____

5. _____

6. _____

7. _____

8. _____

9. _____

10. _____

Finish this sentence: "My favorite client values the products or services I offer because..."

_____

_____

Now, look back at your list. What do you see? The list might be pretty interesting because the items that you write down will probably reflect on both you and your target client profiles. For example, you might have written that your favorite client appreciates that you always follow up in a timely fashion. This might also be what you truly appreciate about your clients as well!

- *My favorite client appreciates my follow-up skills*
- *My favorite client always wants to hear about our latest products and services*
- *My favorite client can't wait to tell me about their latest breakthrough or success story*
- *My favorite client always wants to better themselves*
- *My favorite client is committed to their clients and we share very similar values*

You will probably notice many parallels between what your favorite clients appreciate about you and what you look for in a target client!

Target Clients and the Universal Law of Attraction

The next area we will explore has to do with methods of attracting your target clients to you. Now that you know who they are (a lot like you!), the next step is to figure out how to position yourself so that they will have the opportunity to connect with you. The goal here is to give your target clients the easiest possible access to you. Realistically, if they do not have easy access to you, it will be very difficult for them to say *yes* to your products and services.

Again, this is not to suggest that you need to go out and look for them. In fact, the simplest way to find your target clients is to spend time at places where you enjoy spending time and allow natural attractions and connections to occur. Sounds simple...because it is!

For example, do you have a networking group that you really enjoy attending right now? If so, you are probably already naturally connecting with clients who are great prospects for you. Are there other places or groups that you belong to that you enjoy attending on a regular basis? For example, it might be a hiking club, church, non-profit group, etc. These could all be great places to potentially meet your target clients.

I had a client tell me recently that she really disliked networking with "stuffy" business people. When I asked her if she had to network with "stuffy" business people, she said no but she felt pressured to do so because of the business she was in. In her business, clients did not even have to be business people, but somehow she had pushed herself into a corner to believe that she wasn't a good sales person if she did not connect with business people. After some soul-searching and more questions, she realized that she wanted to network at other places that she enjoyed being — places that were not business-related. When she started networking at these new places, she recognized that there were business people there, but in a different environment, they didn't feel "stuffy" to her.

Why did this occur? Because they were *like* her and they shared the same values. The look on her face was priceless, as a huge "imaginary" weight had been easily lifted from her shoulders! Is there a hobby that you enjoy or a group that you have thought about joining but stopped yourself because you didn't think it would be the "right kind" of networking? Perhaps it is time to take a risk and find out what kind of clients you will attract when you are in places you enjoy, rather than places you feel you should be! This could be at the golf course, the spa, your favorite restaurant, church, etc. Go where you feel good!

> Once you have a list of the qualities you would like your clients to possess, you can then begin to be open to them showing up.

Now that you have a list of the qualities you would like your target clients to possess, you can begin to be open to them just showing up. Yes — just showing up! It's amazing what happens once you are clear on who you would like to show up. The great part is that you will recognize them once they are in front of you.

VISUALIZATION EXERCISE: Close your eyes and envision all of your target clients coming to you. Who did you see? Where did they find you? What has occurred to you?

_____

_____

_____

_____

What do you have to do or let go of in order to attract more target clients? How are you getting in your own way?

_____

_____

_____

_____

_____

$\text{\$}$ INTENTIONAL ACTION

Take a moment and imagine that you are standing in a special room and that your target clients, as you have described them above, are circling you.

Notice that there is an inner circle of your current target clients, and behind them another circle of target prospects, and another circle and on and on as far as your mind will take you.

Feel their positive energy! Listen to their words and what they are saying. See their smiling faces.

This Is What Your Business Could Be Like!

How does it feel to be in the middle of that circle?

Let that energy build up in your chest and explode into the circle around you! Wow!

Now, take a moment and listen to what they are saying about you to each other. Write those words down.

Whatever they are saying is what your target clients probably already say about you!

(Make sure it is positive, and if you hear negative words, do not write those down. Simply ask for the positives!)

When clients begin to talk about you, it will lead to referrals and more referrals. Great opportunities come when your target clients say wonderful things about you to other people.

What do you want your clients to be saying?

Create an Intentional Schedule & Follow It

"So much of our time is spent in preparation, so much in routine, and so much in retrospect, that the amount of each person's genius is confined to a very few hours."

— Ralph Waldo Emerson —

Plan Your Leisure Time First

When I first started out in the business world, I used to purchase day timers with calendars that already had the dates and holidays written in. At the time, I knew the company that I was working for offered a specific number of holidays, and I knew I had limited vacation time, so I just assumed (like a lot of us do) that I would take my two weeks off per year, enjoy a few holidays, and spend the rest of my time working. What a logical decision! Right? Wrong! It took me a long time to realize, first and foremost, that life is short, and second, that I was in control of my life which included my business life *and* my leisure time. Wow, what a concept! Does that ring true for you, or do you find yourself planning your life around your work?

Now, there is absolutely nothing wrong with being a wonderful, loyal employee, so please don't misunderstand me. However, at some point, it is important to think about the priorities in your own life and how they might be compromised if you aren't able to put them first. If you don't take care of yourself, you won't be any good to your company anyway.

When I was the President of the IT company, I would sometimes tell employees that they MUST take their vacation time because it was unhealthy for them to work as much as they did. There were employees who would build their time off past the four weeks they could actually accumulate in a year and literally *not* take time off.

I realized that sometimes people would just get into such a routine that it was almost easier to continue to work than to think about how they would spend their time off. I also realized that many of them didn't have hobbies anymore and had lost touch with those things in life (besides work) that had once fueled them. The worst part was that *I was one of those people.* So as their leader, how could I possibly expect them to exhibit any other behavior if I wasn't willing to take time off myself? (Sound familiar?)

Today I own a day timer that allows me to write all of the dates and holidays in. So I begin my annual scheduling with holidays and time off! That's right! I pencil in my time off first. What a liberating feeling! I challenge you to think about your schedule and how your priorities fit into them. There are many ways that we could all "work smarter" so we could take more time off. What could you do to take control of your schedule, and ultimately your life, today?

I want you to consider the following question: "What is not creating your intentional schedule costing you in your business and personal life?" You might be reading this chapter thinking, "Yes, it would be nice to have an intentional schedule, but what I am doing seems to be working just fine." Taking a good look at your current schedule might help you realize that not having an intentional schedule is costing you a lot.

Do your days often feel like they're getting away from you? Do you get caught up in phone calls, the Internet, and e-mail?

Do you struggle to meet deadlines because there always seems to be something that comes up and needs your attention? If you answered yes to any of these questions, then your lack of an intentional schedule is undermining your #1 priority — selling!

Financially, it is probably costing you a lot because you don't have a schedule and system in place that will keep you on track. On a deeper level, it may be costing you emotionally as well. Lack of a schedule can create unnecessary stress because you end up worrying about the things you should be doing rather than doing them! Procrastination during your workday then leads to a loss of time with your family because you need to make up time somewhere else. Financially, it is probably difficult to quantify exactly how much it might be costing you. However, it's safe to say that creating an intentional schedule and following it will make a significant difference in your pocketbook and your stress levels!

> There are many ways that we could all "work smarter" so we could take more time off.
>
> What could you do to take control of your schedule, and ultimately your life, today?

The Intentional Schedule Formula

I teach my clients to design their intentional schedule by first determining how many vacation days they want to take per year. Now, this will be different for everyone depending on whether you are self-employed or if you work for someone else. If vacation time is a benefit for you, it might be worth it to try and negotiate more vacation time at your next evaluation (provided it is appropriate in that situation for you). If you could wave a magic wand and have as many vacation days as you desired, how many would you want?

Now, take a moment and really think about this! How many vacation days would you take if there would not be any negative repercussions in your life? (After all, you have control of those outcomes!)

I worked with a very successful CEO who was "buried" in his company. He told me he didn't have time to take vacations, and I told him he didn't have a choice. If he didn't start taking time off, his health would further deteriorate and it wouldn't matter if he had a company or not. One year later, he had five vacations planned throughout the year. They'd already been paid for, and his family was eagerly anticipating them. Since then he has started another business because he realized he was even more productive and effective when he took time off! Again, how many vacation days do you choose to take?

$ⁱ INTENTIONAL ACTION

Write down the number of days you want to take off this next year and "X" those days off in your day timer or blackberry.

You heard me — the entire next year!

I have had clients decide they are going to take one week off per month, every Friday off, every Monday off, etc! When you go through this exercise, you begin to realize that you probably do not currently make the best use of your time.

When you build an intentional schedule, you start to build real time management that includes leisure activities that you enjoy and stay in the habit of participating in. Scheduling activities on your weekends, if you get them off, is a great way to ensure that they aren't spent completely on the couch.

In addition to scheduling your vacation days, it is also important to go back through and schedule time for mental and physical health activities. For example, you might want to schedule in your weekly exercise activities.

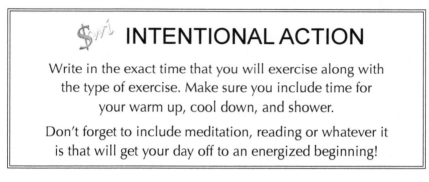

INTENTIONAL ACTION

Write in the exact time that you will exercise along with the type of exercise. Make sure you include time for your warm up, cool down, and shower.

Don't forget to include meditation, reading or whatever it is that will get your day off to an energized beginning!

Schedule your days intentionally so that you will achieve everything on your list for that day.

Now that you have scheduled the time for yourself that will keep you at the top of your game, don't neglect scheduling time with the important people in your life. This might be your spouse, partner, children, or extended family. How much time do you currently spend with them? How much time do you want to be spending with them?

INTENTIONAL ACTION

Write in the time that you will spend with your family and friends on a weekly basis.

Since there will be times when your spouse needs extra time or your child's soccer game comes up suddenly, remember to add a level of flexibility to your schedule to ensure that you can make adjustments smoothly.

Breaking It Down To Your Intentional Day

Next, it is important to evaluate and decide how you would like each workday to be scheduled. If you are going to truly sell with intention, then knowing how your day will go by the hour will be incredibly empowering.

First, decide when you would like to end your day. Yes, begin with the end! Most people today, especially those who own their own businesses or are in sales, work more hours than they want to and find their days dragging into the evening hours. Stop that now! You have already added your leisure activities, vacation days and time with your family into your schedule. Now, decide when you would like to end your workday.

Again, think of it in terms of waving a magic wand and being able to choose exactly when you would end your day. If you choose 4:00p.m., I would encourage you to see what you would have to do to end at 3:00p.m. That way, should anything else come up, you have an hour to work it out.

$ʷⁱ INTENTIONAL ACTION

Write in the time that you will end your day.

Discipline in committing to your intentional schedule will be incredibly important. It just isn't going to happen; you have to make it happen. And once you are committed to an intentional schedule, an intentional schedule, exciting things will begin to happen in your business and in your life. Instead of all of that busy work you have been doing (I hear you laughing!), your hours will be filled with intentional activities designed to take your sales and business exactly where you want them to go!

Okay, so now you know how many hours you will have in your intentional schedule. You know when your day will begin, how it will begin

> If you are going to truly sell with intention, then knowing how your day will go by the hour will be incredibly empowering.

(meditation, exercise, etc.) and when it will end. You also know when and how you will be spending your other available time in terms of leisure activities, hobbies and family time. Your intentional schedule is coming together! The real magic will start to unfold as you build the rest of your schedule hour by hour. Now, you will have the opportunity to determine exactly when you will make your phone calls, schedule your appointments, and meet with your target clients.

At the age of twenty-three, I had the opportunity to open up a new branch for a IT training company. My manager told me that I needed to get the branch to $50,000 per month (revenue!) before I could hire any staff. At the time, I really didn't know any better. I just believed that if I created a daily and weekly schedule that I could stick with, and reached the prospects that I needed to reach, I would reach that first tier goal.

Let me tell you, it wasn't easy driving an hour each way to an empty office, making hundreds of phone calls each morning completely alone, and then going out in the afternoon to meet with prospects to close business, but I stuck to my schedule. Within days, I had already made some phenomenal contacts, and within weeks, the office was delivering business. I reached that first goal of $50,000 per month within just a few months! The lessons I learned, though, were invaluable. Most of all, sticking to my schedule had paid real dividends, and I had reached my goals in less time and with much less effort.

Know and Take Care of Yourself

Schedule your breaks first! Don't you love being intentional about your schedule? You know yourself better than anyone so you know when you need breaks the most. I tend to break around 10:00a.m. and 3:00p.m. for a short time to open up my mind. Or, on some days, that might be the end of my day as well depending on my intentional schedule. Taking a lunch break is especially important because without that, your mind cannot be fueled to continue on with the day. Being intentional about having a healthy meal, where you actually sit down and look at your food before you eat it, will keep your brain working at the level you want it to work. My 10:00a.m. and 3:00p.m. breaks also include a drink and a snack, and I would encourage you to include that as well.

$ᵕⁱ INTENTIONAL ACTION

Schedule your breaks for your intentional day.
(Include lunch, snacks, stretching, etc.)

$ᵕⁱ INTENTIONAL ACTION

Identify your best work hours and the times of day that would make sense for each of the tasks you need to complete.

Are you a morning person? Afternoon? What time of day do you do your best work? Please take a moment to consider these questions because they are very important in terms of deciding when you will do certain activities. I was raised on a working farm, so from a young age I was up very early ready for the day. Today, I still love mornings and do my best work early in the day. I schedule my regular client meetings in the morning or before two in the afternoon.

The afternoon is saved for administrative tasks before I close my day down. I don't even attempt to do real work in the late afternoons or evenings because it ends up being of lower quality. What do you know about yourself in terms of when you do your best work? If you are a morning person, you will want to do your most difficult tasks in the morning. If you are an afternoon person, you will want to perform your difficult tasks later in the day. However, you must also consider your prospects and when you will be able to reach them. Some of your prospects may refuse to meet in the afternoon so you will also need to retain a level of flexibility in your scheduling so you can accommodate those.

However, the goal of the intentional schedule is to have a PLAN that you can follow which can develop a habit to ensure that you are creating as much consistency as possible in your business.

Add Your Intentional Sales Plan to Your Schedule

You have now determined when you do your best work. Remember, this is a skeleton, a structure which should still retain a level of flexibility. Look at your daily schedule again. When do you want to block in time to call or market to your new prospects? In an earlier chapter, you determined how many clients you wanted and how much money you desire to make this year. With this knowledge, you can calculate exactly how many hours you need to work per week and per day to reach your financial goals. Knowing the amount of time you need to reach your goals is the most important place to begin, or the rest of this chapter and creating your intentional schedule will not be useful. Once you have the best formula for you, your intentional schedule can truly transform your personal and professional life!

Intentional Life Formula

- *Intentional Life = Annual Income*

- $\underline{Annual\ Income}$
  Amount of Average Sale = Number of Clients

- *Total Appointments Needed Annually = $\underline{Number\ of\ Clients}$*
  Closing Ratio

- *Appointments Per Week = $\underline{Total\ Appointments\ Needed\ Annually}$*
  Weeks Scheduled to Work

[Closing Ratio = Number of Sales Closed / Number of Appointments]

I've included an example of how this works for one of my clients:

- *Intentional Life = $200,000*

- $\underline{\$200,000}$
  $5,000 Average Sale = 40 Clients

- *120 Appointments Needed Annually = $\underline{40\ Clients}$*
  33%

- *3 Appointments Per Week = $\underline{120\ Appointments\ Needed\ Annually}$*
  40 Weeks Scheduled to Work

[Closing Ratio = 1 Sale Closed / 3 Appointments = 33%]

Next, decide when you want to schedule appointments to meet with your target prospects. Perhaps you will make calls in the morning for two hours per day, two days per week. To be extra intentional, determine how many appointments you intend to set before you make the calls. For example, if you are going to make 20 quality telephone calls to set appointments, you might "intend" to actually set 10 appointments, or 50%.

The other three days of the week, based on your intentional sales formula, you might decide that you need to have three prospect appointments scheduled each day to reach your sales goal. Remember to also add follow-up time to your calendar to get in touch with those prospects that you haven't yet been able to set an appointment with. Go ahead and add those items to your Intentional Schedule.

In another chapter, we will discuss how to connect with intention so you are able to intentionally attract prospects to you. In order to do that successfully, you must be out in places where they can be attracted to you. Sounds simple, and it really is! So, you need to add time into your schedule for making meaningful connections with prospects. Most experts suggest attending no more than four networking events per month. Get involved with organizations that share your values and target clients, and the rest will take care of itself. Perhaps you will belong to one networking group that meets monthly, and two or three others that meet a few times per month. For some of you, the company you work for might have an extensive marketing budget that drives prospects to you, or you might take the cold-calling route. Networking, direct marketing or cold-calling can all be great ways to connect with prospects depending on your industry. Just make sure that you have marked that time off on your intentional schedule for each activity.

$ INTENTIONAL ACTION

Schedule your entire work day — meetings with clients, phone calls, follow-ups, e-mails, administrative tasks, etc.

Are you getting excited yet? You should be! Your plan is almost complete. You have now scheduled your family time, leisure time, hobbies, health rituals and business development schedule. Now, what's left?

The next goal is to turn your intentional schedule into a habit. Studies suggest that it can take up to six weeks to turn activity into a habit. Can you commit the next six weeks to following this schedule with diligence? I hope you are nodding your head yes! Since we are all human, I would suggest that you create a reward for yourself to work toward and enjoy once you reach a goal. The reward can be anything, but it must be motivating enough to you to ensure that you will stay the course. A daily, weekly, and monthly reward system can be even more powerful and I would highly encourage it. Here comes the psychology again!

Psychologists who study behavior rely on B.F. Skinner's behavior conditioning ideas to help their clients reach their goals. Creating your very own token reward system will assist you in staying committed along this journey. Develop a chart for yourself, put it somewhere in your office where you can see it, and actually "X" off the days that you are successful and reward yourself when you reach the goal. I guarantee that if you do this, your intentional schedule will become a tool that you can rely on.

 INTENTIONAL ACTION

Schedule your rewards.

What will you do? Where will you go?

INTENTIONAL ACTION

Go back one more time and look at your schedule.

Does it look realistic?

Do you get excited when you look at it?

If you answered NO to either one of these questions,
then take time to carefully go back through and make
it work for you and your life.

Finally, you have it! The completed intentional schedule! Give yourself a huge pat on the back and thank yourself for taking the time to create a schedule that will make achieving your sales goals simple and straightforward.

Creating and implementing an intentional schedule will make it easier for you to reach your goals. After you have created it, posting in a highly visible area will keep you on track!

Develop Your System for Follow-Up

"Those who are blessed with the most talent don't necessarily out-perform everyone else. It's the people with follow-through who excel."

— Mary Kay Ash —

The Power of Following Up

*A*re you interested in growing your business this year? Most people answer with a resounding yes! Business development is typically at the top of every CEO, VP of Sales, Entrepreneur, and Sales Person's "to do" list at any given moment. If you are ready to really grow your business, one of the main secrets to selling with intention is follow-up!

Most people underestimate the value of following up with their target prospects, current clients, or strategic business partners. It is easy to sit back and believe that if you get your name out there enough times, your phone is just "magically" going to begin to ring. Yes, sometimes that happens, and I believe it happens even more when you are clear on who your target clients are and where you are spending your time; but most likely, you are going to need to follow up with your target prospects regularly before they become clients. And, you are going to need to intentionally follow up with your current clients and strategic business partners if you are expecting any referrals from them.

There are many questions regarding how often a sales person should follow up and how they should do it, but I recommend five keys for follow-up success. Whether it's a networking event or a formal meeting, these keys can help you turn your prospects into clients! If you are at a networking event, though, you can save yourself a lot of time by bringing your day timer and scheduling an appointment in the moment.

Before I get to those keys, take a moment and quantify how many opportunities you have right now to follow up on. Count them. Now, these could be target prospects, current clients, or strategic business partners. Most people have quite a few follow-up opportunities on their desks, day timers, blackberries, e-mails, or to do lists. Sound familiar?

Some of you are actually cringing right now, maybe even feeling a bit nauseous or overwhelmed thinking about all of the opportunities that are available to you at this very moment. It's easy to think, "No, not me." Sometimes we don't even remember the people we have met in the past and the networking opportunities we could have followed up on but didn't. Are you surprised? Just when you thought you didn't have anyone to call or e-mail, it turns out there are quite a few prospects. You probably haven't followed up because you simply don't have a system that works. Well, I am going to share a system with you in a moment.

Before I do that, I want to stress that you do not need to follow up with everyone you meet! Some people do, but I recommend that you make five meaningful intentional connections at each networking (or other) event and follow up with those people. Your goal should be to attract target prospects that match your value system, so make it a goal to evaluate whether

> The goal is meaningful connections that will be worthwhile in the long run, not a bunch of business cards to throw in your drawer when you get home.

or not prospects or business associates fit that mold when you meet them. Remember, sometimes our first impressions can be kind of blurred due to the "glasses" of perception we all wear, so take some time to chat with that person before you ask for their card. The goal is meaningful connections that will be worthwhile in the long run, not a bunch of business cards to throw in your drawer when you get home.

The Five Keys to Follow-Up Success

Key #1 - Schedule

Schedule time to follow up. This sounds pretty simple, right? Yet, most people do not do it, and it is the number one reason why most people don't follow up. I recommend that you block out specific time in your Intentional Schedule so that you have time set aside to regularly follow up. Why? Because if you don't see it on your schedule, it won't get done! I guarantee it! We all know how easy it is to get distracted. E-mail beckons, the Internet calls, or other busy work seems to crop up, and we simply do not make time to follow up. What happens when you actually put it on your schedule? You do it! Wow! There is no magic involved. Statistically, we get 25% more done simply by writing it down. The amount of time that you have on your calendar to follow up should correlate with your Intentional Sales Plan.

We can all have the intention to schedule some time on our day timer or Blackberry and then just never get to it. Why? Because we scheduled it at a time when we get a lot of phone calls or, in general, just get distracted. So, it is very important to choose a time on your weekly schedule when you know you can commit, without question, to following up. Choose a day and time every week when you know you won't be interrupted. Or, if you receive a lot of phone calls or distractions no matter what day it is, commit to yourself that you will not answer your phone or e-mail during this time. This will be difficult for most people, but having a solid commitment to follow up will change your sales results!

---

w^i **INTENTIONAL ACTION**

Schedule a time in your calendar for follow-up each week.

Key #2 — Make the Call or Send the Gift

Okay, so we have to point out the obvious here: You must set your intention and make the call to get the appointment! The actual follow-up is obviously a very important part of the entire process. How you follow up will dictate how you will be remembered, and how you will be remembered directly correlates with whether or not you will hold that prospect or business associate's interest long enough for them to buy. Think unique, think memorable, and be assured that if you have those two components included, you will be remembered!

There are many ways to follow up. The first and most obvious way might be a telephone call. However, if you are going to follow up by phone, you should have a pretty compelling reason to do so. If you discussed having coffee with this person, then following up with a phone call to schedule coffee fairly soon after you met them would be really important. I have seen many people "talk" about getting together but then never follow up to schedule an appointment. Huge mistake! Why? *Because right away you are sending a message that you don't do what you say you are going to do.* When you send that message, people will then apply this to your future behavior (whether or not this is accurate) and assume that you will act the same way in other situations. We will cover exactly what you need to say to get the appointment in Chapter 9.

T. Harv Eker, author of *Secrets of the Millionaire Mind*, says that "how you do anything is how you do everything." I think he's right, and I believe that once people believe you don't do what you say you are going to do, that forever clouds their "glasses" regarding how they see you. So, if you meet someone, and you talk about having coffee with him or her and they are interested in this idea, then follow up with them immediately and make a date for coffee!

Other successful ways to follow up include sending a hand-written note, gift, letter, or e-card that includes how you will follow up next with them. Whatever you say in the note, make sure you schedule it in your activities so you can follow up the way you said you would. Again, credibility in your written word is just as (if not more) important as in your spoken word. After all, they can pick up that hand-written note many times and think, "You know, she never called me back after she said she would."

Another fantastic way to follow up is to ask them if they are interested in receiving the monthly newsletter that your business sends out to keep in touch. That's a phenomenal way to maximize your connection because you will be able to stay in touch with them month after month.

After speaking to a crowd of almost two hundred people, I made some wonderful contacts at an event, and several of them mentioned they would like to meet with me. Others asked to be put on my newsletter distribution list after I offered it to them, and I was able to keep in touch month after month. Six months after the event, a gentleman who had been in the audience and on my newsletter list contacted me. He was ready to meet! Staying connected really will pay off in your sales results. Figure out how you can stay in touch regularly.

$ⁿⁱ **INTENTIONAL ACTION**

List the three primary ways you will follow up.

Key #3 — Update

So, you scheduled time to follow up, you were diligent and determined about how you would follow up, and you took action. Now what? How can you ensure that you stay on the right course of action, and what will you do next? The third key is to update your contact management tool to reflect the actions you took and your plan to stay connected with this specific client. Sounds easy but most people simply are not taking the time to do it, and it really takes away from all of their other effort to follow up. Make sure that you include all pertinent information including their name, address, contact information, where you met them, how you followed up, and what you intend to do next.

It is difficult to make this portion happen if you don't have a decent contact management tool. There are many different options and versions out there, so if you don't currently have one, take the time to evaluate all of the options available. What do you need? Not need? Some of the tools might look very interesting to you because they have a lot of bells and whistles. But unless you will commit to taking the time to understand all of those bells and whistles, it might be better to purchase a software solution that will meet your needs in a simple fashion. Even Outlook has the ability to allow you to schedule your action items and follow-ups. It's not as sophisticated as others out there, but it is better than nothing if you already have it. And once you are in the habit of following up, you can always upgrade to something more sophisticated.

On a weekly basis, I recommend that you print out a list of contacts from your database and enter your follow up items into your Intentional Schedule so that you can effectively follow up with your new contacts the following week. Perhaps you set some appointments or you scheduled time for a telephone conversation. Whatever it is, just make sure you know when and where you need to be to connect with your prospect!

$\$$ꭱꞓ **INTENTIONAL ACTION**

Schedule time to print out your reports and enter your
planned action items into your day timer.

Key #4 — Take Action

Now you have scheduled time to follow up, you have followed up with your new prospects or business associates, and your day timer is full of upcoming activities! Congratulations! This is a phenomenal way to build momentum in your business and create new potential business. The fourth key is to take action on the next steps you created. For example, you might have scheduled coffee with your prospect or a business associate and now have the opportunity to wow them and be memorable!

Remember, you recently met this prospect, so your first meeting should not be "over the top" in terms of trying to convince them to buy your products or services. Rather, this meeting is about connecting with intention, which we will cover in more detail in a later chapter. Your goal should be to ask a lot of questions and really listen to what they are saying. Sometimes we get so caught up in thinking about what we are going to say that we forget how powerful listening can be! So, prior to the meeting, just set your intention that you are going to be yourself and be a great listener. Have great questions. Be a great conversationalist, and allow people to see who you really are. We will go into deeper detail regarding how to close a sale in Chapter 10.

Typically when you take action, you are beyond the follow-up and have scheduled a formal meeting. That being the case, it is critical that you intentionally choose where you are going to meet. Can you remember a time when you had a meeting, maybe you were the client, and you met at a restaurant or coffee shop that was so busy you simply couldn't even concentrate on what you both were saying? The place you meet tells the prospect or business associate a lot about who you are, so remember to think about the image you are trying to project before you get there.

I once met with a prospect at a place I thought would be really appropriate. However, it turned out to be much busier than I had anticipated, and I found it extremely difficult to talk, much less make a meaningful connection. Needless to say, the prospect did not turn into a client. Now, I make it a point to make sure I meet with prospects at upbeat locations that also offer seating in quiet areas that allow for intentional connections to be made!

$ INTENTIONAL ACTION

Think of four of your favorite places to meet your prospects/clients.

Key #5 — Get Results

You have sent the meaningful note or gift. You have followed up with a phone call and set a time to meet for coffee. You chose the perfect place to meet and had a wonderful, meaningful connection. Now what?

Don't forget the fifth key: You must intentionally get results, so the road doesn't stop at connecting with intention! In a later chapter, we will discuss this in more detail. What you need to know right now is that you still need to continue your path of following up to get the results that you desire! Sounds simple, right? If it were so simple, everyone would be doing it.

Unfortunately, sales people sometimes believe that they have done enough once they have delivered the sales presentation of the century. Some are even able to get a signed contract at the first meeting, but I only recommend that if your client has shown you that they are ready to go. You should never, and I mean never, pressure your prospects or clients to make a decision because it is unethical, and when you do that they will likely change their mind anyway. Again, if you don't want to be remembered as the high-pressure sales person, then don't pressure your target prospects. But do give them the next step in the sales process, whatever that might be for your product or service.

So, what can you do? You can send an intentional follow-up note after the meeting that reminds the client of your next appointment. I guarantee that if they are your target prospect and you have made a meaningful connection, they are most likely going to want to purchase your products or services. You just need to make it easy for them to do. Again, at the end of the first meeting, let them know how you will follow up with them and how their options will be presented. Before you leave the meeting, set up a time for your next appointment.

You do not need to discuss price here unless they ask and are ready to buy. You can simply tell them how you will get the information to them (fax, e-mail,

> If you don't want to be remembered as the high-pressure sales person, then don't pressure your clients.

or perhaps your assistant) and then let them know when to expect to hear from you. Ideally, if you are writing a proposal, set another in-person appointment as we discussed above. Be sure to record this in your contact management tool and then follow up with an e-mail confirming the time you will meet. By that time, they will have made a decision, probably in your favor!

Intentional Follow-Up Works

I once attended a networking event and was approached by a prospect who wanted to hear more about my business. At the time, he told me he was going to speak with his boss regarding bringing in additional sales coaching help to take his team to the next level. He asked me to get in touch with him in two months so we could set an appointment prior to his meeting with his boss. I handed him my business card, shook his hand, and told him I would *follow up*. When I got back to my office that day, I crafted a formal follow-up letter, graciously thanked him for taking the time to connect, and gave him some information about the business services that we offer and a few sentences about our success with current clients. The letter closed by telling him I would *follow up* in time to get together prior to his meeting with his boss.

A couple of months later, prior to my scheduled time to call him, I had a voicemail waiting for me. The target prospect told me that he was ready to meet. I called him back immediately, set the appointment for the following week, and arrived with excitement and enthusiasm. As I settled into his office for the meeting, I noticed a letter posted on his board above his computer. *It was the letter I had written following our first connection.*

Greetings Mr. Smith,*

It was a pleasure to connect with you at the local business networking event on Friday and to learn about the goals you have set for you and your team in 2006. Impressive! I can really tell how much you enjoy working for "ABC Company". As I explained on Friday, our clients value their teams and want to double or triple their sales with ease and grace — your organization represents that type of culture!

Our clients experience excellent results in striving for and reaching their <u>highest</u> goals. We attribute that to our ability to help clients get out of their own way. We use performance-based coaching methods that make success happen with *less effort and in less time.* Imagine a year filled with less stress on your part AND *faster results*! In fact, *Potential Quest, Inc.* recently helped a company double their sales in less than two months! We would love to have the opportunity to help your organization achieve the same results.

Please expect a follow-up call no later than August 30th, 2005.

Have an excellent week!

Best Regards,
Ursula Mentjes
President and Certified Sales Coach

*Names and other information have been changed to protect the privacy of the parties involved.

Never underestimate the power of a strong follow-up. Prospects want to know how much you want to do business with them. If you aren't committed to even getting an appointment with them, they may wonder how you will service them if they do become clients. How you follow up tells a prospect what the rest of your relationship will be like. So, impress them with your intentional follow-up so you have the opportunity to impress them with your products or services!

Tracking Your Progress

Your goal should be to make a habit out of following up so that you can keep in touch with your prized prospects and current clients. Using the five keys above, develop your own system to effectively track your prospective clients to keep you moving in the direction of your sales goals. Taking the time to appropriately track the contacts that might turn into strategic partners is also incredibly important. However you decide to do it, just make it yours, and make it work!

There are many ways to measure your sales success, from simple spreadsheets to more sophisticated systems like Customer Relationship Management software. Whatever you decide to use, just be sure that you invest in a tool that allows you to keep track of your sales on a daily, weekly, monthly, and annual basis.

An easy way to get started with sales tracking is to add your top 25 prospects to an excel spreadsheet. Beneath that, add in those prospects that are 99% closed and then add your closed sales below. If you have a difficult time choosing your top 25 prospects, focus on the 80/20 rule.

The 80/20 rule is also referred to as the Pareto Principle because it was discovered by Wilfried Pareto. We can apply the Pareto Principle to sales to realize that 20% of customers contribute 80% of sales and revenue. Usually the top 20% are also your favorite clients — the clients that are extremely loyal and a joy to work with! The key, then, is to focus on getting more clients like that. Your top 25 should fit the profile of your top 20%!

A good guide might be to separate them into three categories on a weekly and monthly basis: Your closed sales, sales that are 99% closed, and prospects. If you keep track on a regular basis, you will begin to see a trend in your reporting. Your target clients will begin to show up in the bottom of the report — in the "closed sales" section. Measuring your results is the only way to build a strong and successful sales pipeline.

TAKE A QUANTUM LEAP

For practical application — to really transform your thoughts and habits — visit www.SalesCoachNow.com and order your copy of our Selling With Intention workbook today.

For ongoing sales training and support, join our growing online community at www.MySalesCoachNow.com.

Educate Your Partners & Clients

"If you have knowledge, let others light their candles with it."

— Winston Churchill —

Who Needs to Know Your Business?

Who needs to knows your business? Strategic business partners, current clients, and prospects need to know your business in order for it to grow. However, before they can understand your product or service, you must know your business at an even deeper level. You need to be clear on the problem you solve, what makes you unique and memorable, and the reason for all of your previous clients' successes. Identifying, clarifying, and communicating those elements in a captivating Intentional 30-Second Introduction will give you the foundation you need to make sure that your strategic business partners, current clients, and target prospects not only know your business, but begin to "sell" for you.

In business we often hear the same old adage, "It's who you know." Well, I can tell you, I know a lot of people, but I'm not sure that they all know me. I'm certain that they don't know my business the way that I would like them to know it. At the same time, I recognize that teaching people about my business is an ongoing process that happens over time.

A few years ago, I was attending a networking event, and someone stood up and said, "It's not who you know, it's who knows you." Since then, I have heard several other people say the same thing, and it really resonated with me. After all, who purchases your products and services? Is it the people you know? Or is it the people who know your products or services? I would venture to guess that it is the people who know your products or services.

How can we encourage people to get to know our products and services? The first step is to make sure that you have a clear message that you feel good about and that is easy for others to understand. Do you have an Intentional 30-Second Introduction that concisely explains the problems that you solve for your clients? It is important to begin with the Intentional 30-Second Introduction because that language will help you design your sales script, voicemail script, and additional marketing materials.

Your Intentional 30-Second Introduction

Let's take a moment to address the Intentional 30-Second Introduction. This is useful whether you are attending a lot of networking meetings or simply trying to explain what you do when speaking with prospects or business associates. I strongly encourage all of my clients to have a crystal clear 30-Second Introduction — one that can be modified at a moment's notice but has a clear foundation. You want it to be flexible, not rigid, so that it will be useful in different settings.

The key to a successful Intentional 30-Second Introduction is to be very intentional in terms of the result that you want to create when you deliver your message. In other words, what do you want people to do after they hear your message? Ask for an appointment? Inquire about your product or service? Whatever it is, be intentional and clear on what you want them to do ahead of time.

Now, it is time to develop your highly effective Intentional 30-Second Introduction with a step-by-step process.

Sales Coach Now

Where Mindset Meets Intention

The 30-Second Introduction Worksheet

When I am attending different networking events, I hear many different introductions, but those that I remember clearly are memorable because they leave me wanting to connect with that person to hear more.

There are six key areas to focus on when creating a 30-Second Introduction that can help make it shine.

First, be intentional about your 30-Second Introduction and know exactly what you want the result to be before you open your mouth. Do you want someone to come up and ask you more about your business? Do you want someone to set up an appointment with you? Whatever you want them to do, make sure that your language is geared toward that result. NLP Practitioners teach that communication is the result that you get. Keep that in mind when you determine what you include in your message.

Second, open up with an attention grabber! Do you have a favorite quote that represents your business? *"Eleanor Roosevelt once said, 'You must do the thing you think you cannot do.'"*

_____

_____

_____

_____

Third, give your name and the company you are with. *"My name is Ursula Mentjes, and I am the President of Sales Coach Now."*

_____

_____

_____

Next, state who your target clients are and how you help them solve problems. *"I work with sales professionals and entrepreneurs who are tired of dealing with a lack of sales and opportunities."*

_____

_____

_____

Then, tell a recent success story that will help people better understand the results they will achieve by purchasing your product or service. *"I help business leaders get out of the comfort zone so they can double or triple their sales. I just recently helped several Account Executives at a Fortune 500 company double and triple their monthly sales results."*

_____

_____

_____

_____

Finally, close your 30-Second Introduction with a statement that people will remember and associate only with you, and leave them wanting more. *"I guarantee 100% satisfaction or your money will be refunded in full! My name is Ursula Mentjes, and I am the President of Sales Coach Now."* Put it all together so it flows!

_____

_____

_____

Success Tips

1. To ensure that your message is clear, practice your Intentional 30-Second Introduction in front of a mirror so it flows flawlessly.

2. You might also want to ask your business associates and team members if you can practice in front of them and then solicit feedback from them.

3. While you are perfecting it, think about what you want your prospects or referral partners to do after you

> Remember, the more people that know, the more your business will grow!

deliver your 30-Second Introduction. Do you want them to take action? Come and talk to you? Whatever it is, keep checking in to make sure your message consistently does these things.

4. Check in with your energy level prior to delivering the Intentional 30-Second Introduction. Make sure you deliver it with a smile and lots of energy or all of your hard work will fall on deaf ears.

5. Finally, make sure your intention is clear before you arrive at the event or to a prospect meeting. Be intentional about what you know you want to happen before you leave the event and who you want to connect with.

Are You Memorable?

If you spend time carefully crafting your Intentional 30-Second Introduction, and practice it until it is natural, you will become memorable. If you'd like to be even more memorable, then you need to choose success stories that will resonate with the audience or individuals you are in front of. When I share success stories, people come over and talk to me to find out more. For example, I helped a Real Estate company increase sales by 40% in just 30 days during the recession. That story moves people into action!

They say that people remember how you made them feel, not what you did. So you can actually set yourself apart and be memorable just by treating other people with respect and truly connecting with them.

In a sea of many businesses, you or your business must be unique enough to stand out from the crowd. Think about a business that you feel is really unique. What is it about that business that makes it special?

> When is the last time that you made someone feel really important? Think about it. Remember it. Because that was the last time you were memorable.

Many times they aren't that different from their competitors, but they have found a way to stand out and they are willing to go above and beyond to do so.

One of my strategic business partners, a very talented esthetician, is extremely unique. While you are relaxing and enjoying an incredible facial, she just "throws in" a hand massage, foot massage, shoulder massage and head massage. Pretty unbelievable, right? Let's just say that it is easy to refer people to her because I just happen to mention that in addition to receiving an incredible facial, I am also treated to a hand, foot, shoulder and head massage. Before I can even offer her card, people are asking me for it. She goes above and beyond, and that makes her memorable. The key is to make sure that whatever makes you unique and memorable is not your best kept secret. Others must know about it.

$wi INTENTIONAL ACTION

Identify what makes you memorable or unique.

Who Knows Your Business Today?

Being intentional about others knowing your business must include a reality check. How many clients or business associates today really know your business or what you sell? And I mean, REALLY know your business. Even if these people are currently clients, that doesn't necessarily mean that they know everything they need to know about the products or services that you offer. For example, if a client knows about one of your services and has purchased it, but doesn't know about the other services that you offer, then they really don't know your business. And, they might be interested in buying more from you!

So, you ask, "How do you know if someone really knows your business?" Great question! You know because they refer business to you. They know your business so well that they can actually articulate to someone else what it is that you do or what you sell. And once they give the referral, it's so strong that the person calls you because they are interested in doing business with you based on what they were told by their trusted colleague. Do you have clients or strategic partners like that right now? If not, it is time to begin to educate your current clients and prospects in a way that will help them remember what you do or what you sell.

Give Them the Language

To have others articulate what you do or what you sell as well as you do is the highest compliment. It means that you are truly out there networking and helping others in a way that is memorable. I challenge you to take some time to think about this, though. What do you really want others to say about you or your products or services? How do you want them to sell your business to others? You need to give them the words.

Set appointments with your strategic partners to share the elements of your Intentional 30-Second message and your success stories, and then strategize on how you can best help each other.

$ **INTENTIONAL ACTION**

Imagine that you are standing in front of your favorite strategic business partners. Ask them to describe in one sentence the product or service you offer and the problem it solves. What do they say?

Write it down. Look at it. Is it the message that you want to have out there? What would you change about it?

Share Your Products or Services

How can you encourage people to talk positively about your business to others? Above, we discussed how to be unique and memorable. But if you really want to get people talking, you must go even beyond the boundaries of being unique and memorable. How? Simple. They need to try your products or services.

Think about a time when someone was trying to convince you how great their product or service was. Do you remember what that felt like? When someone is trying to convince us, we usually tune out. A friend of mine was raving about a new product that she loved that was supposed to take inches off your body. I didn't believe her. She kept trying to convince me and finally another friend invited me to her house to try it. So I did. And then I was hooked. Prospects need to try your products or services to become believers. When they believe, they will buy from you *and* they will tell others.

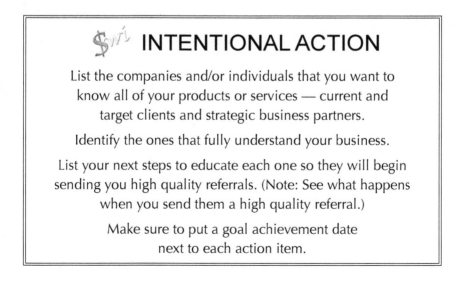

INTENTIONAL ACTION

List the companies and/or individuals that you want to know all of your products or services — current and target clients and strategic business partners.

Identify the ones that fully understand your business.

List your next steps to educate each one so they will begin sending you high quality referrals. (Note: See what happens when you send them a high quality referral.)

Make sure to put a goal achievement date next to each action item.

Connect With Intention

"I don't care how much you know until I know how much you care."

— Author Unknown —

Selling With Intention = Connecting With Intention

*P*lease read this chapter carefully, and refer back to it whenever you feel stuck in your your sales results. As you read this book, you will see that *connecting* with intention is at the core of *selling* with intention. If you don't connect intentionally, the rest of the information in this book is useless. Connecting with intention at a basic level means building rapport by being your most authentic self. But even more than that, connecting with intention means building rapport and establishing heartfelt connections with your prospects, clients, and strategic business partners, and truly caring about their success. If you always remember those two points, your sales career will flourish beyond your greatest dreams.

Let's begin with what it means to develop rapport with your prospects. What is rapport? Rapport is defined as *"relation, connection, especially harmonious or sympathetic relation"* according to the *American Heritage Dictionary.*

Rapport is the trust and agreement that you must create with your prospect before you will ever have an opportunity for your relationship to grow. Second, a feeling of empathy means that you are getting at the core of what your prospect is feeling. In other words, you are stepping into their shoes and standing in their world. You are putting on the glasses of their worldview so you can see how the world looks to them. It promotes a level of compatibility between you and your prospect. This does not mean that you are suddenly best friends, but it means that you can begin to talk to each other on a more meaningful level regarding what is going on in their business and how you might be able to solve their problems and provide a meaningful solution.

Building Rapport

Now that we have defined it, how can you build rapport effectively? Neuro-linguistic programming, or NLP, teaches that you can effectively build rapport with someone by matching and mirroring their body language in addition to matching their breathing and rate of speech. Not only will this make the prospect feel even more comfortable, it will also give you a chance to more fully step into their world.

Mirroring and matching will give you a whole new idea of the state your target prospect is currently in, which will help you understand how you might be able to help them. When you add in matching their breathing, you will find that you are connecting with them exactly where they are in that moment. And when you are connecting with intention, the prospect will have the opportunity to be honest with you and more openly explain their current situation and needs. I encourage my clients to imagine there is a bubble around them so the other person feels their full attention when they are connecting at networking events.

Now that you can see the power of matching and mirroring your client or prospect to build rapport, it is time to examine and practice the art of listening. I believe that listening is an art. Like other forms of art, one must practice it in order to master it. Many people believe that they are good listeners, when in reality they simply are not.

> Connecting with intention means establishing heartfelt connections with your prospects, and truly caring about their best interests.

As humans, we spend a lot of time in our heads thinking about the next thing we are going to say rather than really listening to what the person in front of us is saying. Now, I'm not saying that you shouldn't think about what you say before you say it, but if you pay close attention to what your prospect is sharing and continue to ask meaningful questions, your prospect will see you as an excellent conversationalist and business person. Most importantly, remember to be yourself throughout this process! Prospects can sense your level of authenticity and will buy from you if they feel the connection is real.

Where Should You Connect?

The ideal situation is to be able to connect with your prospect in person. This could be at a networking event or other industry function. Consider the kinds of events at which your target prospects spend their time. You can make the best use of your time if the majority of people who are at an event are your target prospects.

Choosing the best places to network is critical if networking is an important part of your Intentional Sales Plan. When I first began networking actively, I tried out many different groups before I chose a key few. I can remember that one group, in particular, felt very cold and unwelcoming. Although I made a few great contacts there, the reality was that it just wasn't a good fit. If it's not a good fit, cut your losses early and move on. When I just let go of that group, I made room for others that were a better fit for me. Focusing on a few key groups also gave me the free time I needed to take on leadership positions in organizations that I really cared about. If you are going to spend a lot of time in an organization, find out if you can join their Board of Directors because that will allow you to get the most out of it. As a Board Member, you can deepen and strengthen your relationships with others.

There are a few points of clarity on networking groups that need to be addressed. Just because a certain group isn't a good fit for you doesn't mean that they are a bad group or that they won't be a great fit for someone else. Also, remember that it can take a few weeks for you to warm up to a group and for them to warm up to you, so make sure you give it enough time to make an educated decision. Finally, and most importantly of all, if you expect to receive referrals from people in the group, give referrals first! The more you give, the more that will come back to you if you are open to it.

Before you attend an event like this, I highly recommend that you set your intention regarding how many meaningful connections you would like to make. You know who your target prospects are, so adding this component to your intentional connection plan is really important. Once you are clear on your intention regarding how many prospects you would like to make an intentional connection with at the event, I would then encourage you to check internally to make sure that is what you'd really like to happen. Sometimes when we set our intention, we believe that the logic in our heads is reality. However, when we check in our hearts or in our gut, it might not be in agreement. In fact, we may actually have another intention entirely. Let me give you an example.

Imagine you have a networking event coming up at 5:00p.m. You tell yourself that you are clear on wanting to make five meaningful, intentional connections. At 4:45p.m., you arrive at the event believing that you are clear on why you are there. You then start to make the rounds, but the first few connections you make are awkward and you definitely don't feel like you are making meaningful connections. At 5:30p.m., your spouse calls to see what time you will be home because it is your son's birthday and you are meeting for dinner at 6:00p.m. You knew you could only be at the event for an hour, and during the entire hour, you felt rushed and did not feel like you were connecting. Why not? Because in your heart, you were at home with your family. In reality, it would have been a better use of your time to skip the event so you could arrive early and not feel rushed while honoring your family and your son's birthday party.

If your heart isn't into a networking event, meaningful connections will not happen naturally, so be very clear on your internal state. Otherwise, you might believe a networking event was "bad" when it was really your inability to connect due to other obligations. People will sense if you are focused on your internal world because you will have a very difficult time listening and connecting.

How Will You Know?

So, how will you know when you are truly connecting with intention? You will know because you will be out of your head and you will be listening from your heart. You will be matching your prospect's posture and breathing so rapport will be built quickly. The needs of the prospect and who they are will become abundantly clear because you will be genuinely focusing on them.

On the flip side, how will you know if you aren't connecting with intention? Or, that this isn't the best target prospect for you? You probably won't know at first. However, your job isn't to quickly judge because you could be wrong. Instead, your job is to remain connected and listening to assess whether or not this person is someone you can help. If the connection isn't happening, it could be that you are in your head rather than in your heart, and this prospect is still possibly a target client or strategic partner for you. If you are also thinking about how this deal or prospect could positively impact your business, *and not how you could impact the life of the person in front of you,* then you aren't connecting with

> If you are also thinking about how this deal or prospect could positively impact your business, and not how you could impact the life of the person in front of you, then you aren't connecting with intention.

intention. There will be many clues both ways, so it is up to you to navigate this maze and figure out whether or not this prospect will be one of your five connections for the evening.

Recently, a business acquaintance of mine asked me if I would like to have coffee. I agreed and assumed that the meeting would center on sharing information about our businesses so we could figure out how to support each other as strategic business partners. So, when I sat down at the coffee shop, I was very interested in connecting with intention from the perspective of a potential strategic business partner rather than thinking that this was a potential target client for my business.

As we were sitting there, I was listening as he described his business and his target clients. I continued to listen and ask questions because I wanted to understand exactly what he did in the event that I connected with someone who could utilize his products and services. He then asked me to tell him about my business, so I shared my intentional message, which always includes the problem that I solve for my clients. When I finished explaining, he asked me, "Do you think you could help me do that (sell more) in my business?"

What? I was floored because I wasn't expecting him to ask me this question at all! In fact, my intention had not been to connect with him as a prospect. Quite the contrary! What I did realize, though, was that when you are connecting with intention, you are always selling, even if that isn't your intention! Imagine how different your business will become when you are connecting with intention on a regular basis!

Connecting with intention over the phone isn't much different than connecting with intention in person. The main difference is that you obviously can't physically see the person, but you can certainly visualize them in your mind's eye. In addition, you can still match their rate of breathing and talking over the phone so you can get into their current state. Even more importantly, you are still practicing your active listening skills and continuing to ask all the right questions so you can learn about your prospect. The challenge over the phone is to not become distracted and drift away from the conversation simply because they are not in front of you.

Begin applying the basic principles of connecting with intention and you will be on track to developing strong rapport with your prospects, clients, and strategic business partners. The most important goal of the phone conversation should be to schedule an appointment in person once you have established rapport. Explain to the prospect that your goal is to meet with them in person to demonstrate how your solution can solve the problems they have shared with you. In the next chapter, we will discuss actually setting the appointment, and what to say to move the relationship from a solid connection to an in-person meeting.

Transform Your Business Through Connections

There are many benefits to connecting with intention that can transform your business. First, connecting with intention gives a relationship the foundation it needs to begin to grow. Second, when you connect with intention, you are coming from a place of honesty and integrity because you have the

> When you are connecting with intention, you are ALWAYS selling, even if that isn't your intention!

best interest of the prospect in mind. Third, when you are focused on connecting with intention, you will worry less about whether or not this is a target prospect, and more about who this person is as a human being. Finally, starting from this perspective will give you long-term relationship with whomever you connect, rather than just a transaction.

In addition to some of the benefits of connecting with intention already discussed, it will also transform your business in other ways. As I stated in my illustration above, when you are connecting with intention with everyone you come into contact with, you will develop new clients when you aren't even thinking about it! People will be attracted to your passion for your business, clear message, and obvious interest in delivering real solutions to your clients. People also care more about how you made them feel than what you did for them, and they will remember that, maybe for the first time, someone really listened to them. You will definitely be remembered so that the next time you see them they will want to connect with you.

One specific point that I want to make to ensure that you don't feel bad when you don't connect is that *you won't always make a connection*. There, I said it! It's out! I wish that everyone I connected with turned into a meaningful connection, but that's just not the case. Remember, your goal is to connect intentionally with people who resonate with who you are. This will happen naturally when you are paying attention to being yourself. Not everyone will like you, and not everyone is a good fit for you or your business. However, connecting with intention is a sorting process and, in the end, the best opportunities for you will become clear.

Connecting with intention will set the stage for everything you will ever do with your target prospect. As we all know, most people make first impressions pretty quickly and decide whether or not this person fits into their schema of who they will or will not connect with. If you are matching and building rapport, you will at a minimum be given the opportunity to connect. During those first few minutes, when you are out of your head and listening intently to what the prospect is saying, they will always remember their first impression of you in a positive way, so this will most likely be their point of reference for you.

After you have built the relationship and they have hired you and your company, it will still be important for you to continue to connect with intention. When you do this, you will continue to keep their best interest in mind and heart as your client, and they will be getting the results that you committed to helping them achieve with your products or services. They will appreciate your services so much that they will begin to send you high-quality referrals that will also catapult your business to the next level. Your satisfied clients will usually choose you over the competition and utilize whatever new services you offer. Finally, you will become their trusted consultant and they will rely on you to refer other high-quality professionals to them. When you are able to refer other strategic partners to your clients who trust you, congratulate yourself because your business is at an entirely new level!

$ⁿ⁄ INTENTIONAL ACTION

Think of a time when you connected with intention.

Then think of a time when you didn't.

Looking back on these two experiences, what were some of the obvious differences — type of meeting, energy level, etc.?

Imagine how connecting with intention
will transform your business...

Make a commitment to connecting with intention.

THE NINTH PRINCIPLE

Get the Appointment

"We can do anything we want to do if we stick to it long enough."

— Helen Keller —

Getting the Appointment

*A*t the beginning of my sales career, I believed that if I could get in front of a prospect, I could close business. I still believe that. I also believe that if I can get in front of a target prospect, I can create a long-term mutually beneficial relationship that will take their business to the next level. Now, that does not mean that I decide to work with every target prospect I meet with, because I might determine (or they might) that it is not the right fit. However, if it is a target prospect, and I know that I can dramatically impact their business, I am going to work pretty darn hard to get that appointment. *And you should too.*

I'm going to focus on closing sales and making deals happen in a later chapter. The focus of this chapter is getting the appointment. If you cannot get the appointment, you cannot close a sale. And yet, for most people, asking for an appointment can be just as intimidating as asking for the business. When you think about asking for the appointment, what kinds of images or feelings come up for you? Do visions of cold-calling dance in your head? Does a feeling of nausea crawl up in the pit of your stomach? Well, fear no more! My goal is to take the pain out of getting the appointment by changing the way you think about getting appointments!

Let's take a moment and look at what getting the appointment really is and is not. Getting the appointment is not getting the sale. The best perspective you can hold regarding getting the appointment is that it is an opportunity for you to evaluate whether or not you would like to have this person or business as your client, assuming that they are a good fit for your product or service, and for the prospect to decide whether or not they think you can actually solve their problem (and whether or not they like you!). Think about that for a minute. What if that was your perspective regarding every target prospect in your database?

If you knew that you did not have to close a sale, but just determine if they are a target client, could that take the pressure off of the sales call? How does asking for the appointment look and feel to you now? Different? Easier? The reality is that it is time for you to take an active approach to developing your client base. You no longer need to let your prospects decide if and when they need your products or services. No! Now it is your turn to evaluate whether or not *you* would like to work with this prospect over the long-term. *You* determine whether or not they are a good fit for your products or services!

I hear you protesting! And I value your protests because you are saying, "Yes, but...I need sales every month, so who the prospect is really does not matter, right?" Wrong! Who your prospect is does matter!

> The best perspective on getting the appointment is that it is an opportunity for YOU to evaluate whether or not YOU would like to have this person or business as your client.

Your Business Basket

What if your "business basket" were overflowing with shiny red apples that all looked, smelled and tasted the same? In my experience, just one sour apple in your basket can ruin the whole bunch. In other words, if you have one or two clients who are not a good fit for your business, they can drain the life and energy out of you. Being drained leaves you less time and energy to prospect, have meetings, and service your other "shiny apples". This kind of distraction can cause you to begin to question everything, and you will be so worn out from those clients, you might begin to wonder why you even got into your industry in the first place. At that point, just think how much those sour apples have cost you!

On the flip side, if you choose to work with an entire basket full of shiny apples, what do you think your business life would be like? Exciting? Inspiring? How will this excitement and positive energy impact the rest of your clients? They might refer you more prospects. You will more easily be able to sell more of your products and services to these excited clients. The list goes on! Wonderful and powerful energy will then begin to spill over into your personal life. You will have more energy for your spouse and your children. You will also have more energy to plan exciting vacations that might also lead to even greater energy and excitement. Do you see where this is going?

I was promoted in 1997 from an outside sales position selling IT training in Denver to a selling sales/branch manager of the Colorado Springs branch. The Colorado Springs branch was new, and I had been promoted to grow it from $0 in revenue per month to the first tier of consistently reaching $50,000 per month. I knew this would not be easy, but I loved sales and was up for the challenge. However, the question was: *How was I ever going to reach the revenue goals fast enough to ensure that the new branch was profitable?*

To begin, I did what I knew I had to do. I started cold-calling and setting appointments. When I use the term "cold-calling", I mean picking up the phone, dialing, making connections, and setting the appointment. For those of you who have cold-called, you know that if you are diligent and focused, you can get a lot of dials in, successfully close appointments, and make some sales. It seems that in recent years, the art of the cold-call has been lost as people want simpler and faster ways to "get clients", but I still believe it can be effective *when done intentionally*. It was extremely effective for me during those first weeks and months of opening the branch when I didn't know anyone in the community.

The positive part was that I was alone in the office in the beginning, so there weren't any distractions when I was making the phone calls. The downside was that it could be very difficult to maintain a high level of motivation and enthusiasm because I didn't have anyone around to support me. I stayed motivated by focusing on the overall monthly goal that I knew I had to reach to take the branch to the next level.

Every morning when I arrived, I printed my call sheet out for the day. Next, I set my intention on what I wanted to achieve out of every call that I made. Internally, I set my intention that I would earn the business of every company in Colorado Springs. (Yes, a lofty goal, but I had nothing to lose!) With that intention, if the prospect didn't immediately want to set an appointment with me, I would still keep them on my prospect list. However, the reality was that when I had the intention to get the appointment, and I told the prospect that my goal was to *earn their business*, it was amazing how those three words truly encouraged people to meet with me! My close rate for appointments was extremely high, and as long as I landed the meeting, I had the opportunity to make a meaningful connection and, ultimately, earn the prospect's business.

Let Go of Fear

So let us travel full circle — back to you getting the appointment with your top prospects. Remember, an appointment is your opportunity to evaluate whether or not that prospect is a good fit for your products or services. The best way to get the appointment is to *ask*! As simple as it sounds, as sales people, we can often give ourselves a million reasons why we won't get the appointment. Fear can take over and before you know it, you might have talked yourself out of setting the appointment.

Many of my clients rate fear as the number one thing that gets in the way of scheduling appointments. It is easy to blame not making appointments on procrastination or time management issues, but usually fear is at the root of it. As human beings, we have a fundamental need to be connected to others and not rejected. When we get rejected, it is easy to question our value and self-worth at a core level. But the reality is that we must learn to not take appointment rejection personally. It is not personal. People have many reasons for not taking an appointment with you. Now, that's not to say that you might not need to tweak your approach, and learn from the experiences — but you can't let it derail you.

If you continually have fear issues that arise, you might need to investigate them at a deeper level. Ask yourself, *What is the fear really about? And how is it impacting the way I interact with my prospects?* If you aren't aware of how those fears are affecting you, they will continue to impact your level of success. Prospects will sense your fear, even if it is over the phone. When they sense your fear, they might say no to you simply because they notice a lack of self-confidence. Unfortunately, no one wants to do business with someone who isn't confident. We do business with the person who has the most genuine confidence and has convinced us that they really can solve our problem.

It will not matter how many hours you put in, how many appointments you set up, or how intentionally you connect or follow up with your prospects. If you do not let go of your fears, those fears will somehow sabotage your success. Have you ever reached the end of a sale where you did everything right, and when the time came to ask for the business, you froze or tripped over your words? Maybe your fear kept you from giving your prospect the opportunity to say yes. Maybe it kept you from displaying the confidence every prospect wants to see in someone they are going to buy a service or product from.

$ INTENTIONAL ACTION

First, you must identify what the fear is really saying to you. Listen to it. There is so much chatter going on in our heads every day that, unless we tune in to it, we aren't even aware of the damaging things that we are telling ourselves. Once you tune in, you might begin to realize that the critical voices you are hearing aren't even yours! The critical words might actually be coming from a parent, teacher, or other authoritarian figure in your life that had been overly critical of you in the past. Their words might have held so much power over you that they are still "real" for you today.

As you hear those words, write them down. Look at them. Evaluate them. Are they your words? Are they from someone else? Most importantly, how do these words serve you today? Most of the time, they don't serve you at all. They might have had a positive intention in the beginning. Perhaps in some way they kept you "safe" because you were protecting yourself from rejection, but now their purpose is getting in the way of your success. Hear the words, write them down, and check in regarding their truth or lack thereof, and then give yourself permission to let them go.

When you can create a habit of letting go of the words or phrases that no longer serve you, you will begin to free yourself to have full success.

As you let your fears go, focus on all of the appointments that you can now schedule. Think about all of the opportunities that are currently available to you. What would your business be like if you were able to put fear aside and delve into the great opportunities that are out there and set appointments with the clients you really want? Your business would be able to grow exponentially and you would be free! Making cold calls or setting appointments would suddenly come from a place of courage and success, rather than a place of fear. Your connections would be intentional and prospects would have the opportunity to see that you have their best interest in mind, and would be much more likely to say yes to an appointment with you!

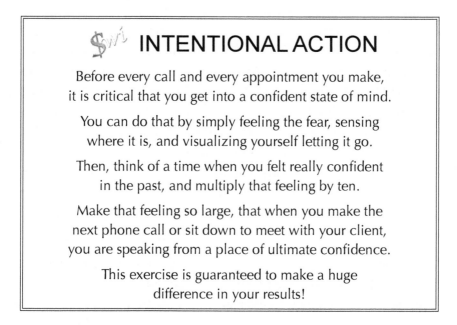

INTENTIONAL ACTION

Before every call and every appointment you make,
it is critical that you get into a confident state of mind.

You can do that by simply feeling the fear, sensing
where it is, and visualizing yourself letting it go.

Then, think of a time when you felt really confident
in the past, and multiply that feeling by ten.

Make that feeling so large, that when you make the
next phone call or sit down to meet with your client,
you are speaking from a place of ultimate confidence.

This exercise is guaranteed to make a huge
difference in your results!

Set the Appointment the Intentional Way

With fear out of the way, it is important to think about the most intentional way to set an appointment. Both your verbal and nonverbal communication are extremely powerful, so being mindful of how you come across to the prospect will make it easier to schedule high quality appointments. It is also important to check in and make sure that you don't come across as over powering either. Prospects will not set an appointment with someone they view as a "know it all" or overly pushy. Remember, the intentional connection must come before you can make the appointment. If you haven't made that kind of connection first, you will know because getting the appointment will not happen in a smooth fashion. Once you have connected with intention, then you can simply ask for the appointment.

Asking in a way that gives the prospect an opportunity to choose an appointment time rather than just say *no* is critical. After all, even after you have made a very positive connection, people are still busy, so the knee-jerk reaction for most people is to say *no* to an appointment. Your goal should be to give them the opportunity to say *yes*! How do you do that? Simple. You open your calendar and you say, "I am available to meet with you next Tuesday or Thursday. Which day works best for you?" When they tell you that Thursday works best, you can then ask them if mornings or afternoons are better. If they say afternoons, you can follow up with, "Great, I can meet with you at 1:00p.m. or 4:00p.m. Which time works best for you?" They will choose the time that works best, and bingo, you have an appointment!

If you are calling your prospect to set the appointment and you only met them briefly, then begin by reminding them of what you discussed when you met. Conversationally, mention the problem that you solve and a recent success story if you can work it in. Remember, this is why your Intentional 30-Second Introduction is so valuable! It is the foundation of your appointment-setting script. If you get voicemail, you can also leave this message to set the appointment. The only difference would be to let them know when you will be available for them to call you back that same day. Give them a two or three hour window of time along with your phone number. Repeat your phone number and remember to speak slowly. Whenever I teach this method in class, my students don't initially believe me. However, after we practice calling in class (yes, real calls!) and they leave voicemails that get returned, they become believers!

After you set the appointment, I encourage my clients to follow up with something fun like, "I will be stopping at a coffee shop before your appointment and would like to treat you to a specialty coffee drink or whatever you would like. What is your favorite drink?" Or, whatever you can think of that is creative that you can treat your prospect to. After all, they are taking time out of their busy day to meet with you. Make it special, and they will actually be looking forward to your meeting and you will be even more memorable.

If you get a flat out *no*, don't despair. Several things could be at play. First, you might not have taken enough time to develop an intentional connection with this prospect, so check in there first. If you feel like this might be the case, close your day timer, take a deep breath, and smile at your prospect. In the last chapter, we discussed the importance of matching a person's posture, breathing, and actions to ensure that you are building rapport. Go back to the basics at this point and match your prospect. Rather than making them defensive by continuing to ask for the appointment, simply begin the rapport-building process again and connect with them.

Be present and say, "I'm sorry. I misunderstood and thought that you might be interested in having a meeting to further explore how I might be able to help you achieve _____ in your business. Please don't feel pressured to meet. Tell me, what results would you have to achieve in order to believe that investing in _____ (your business) would be beneficial to you?"

This takes the pressure off of the prospect in terms of them feeling like they must set an appointment, and instead opens up the dialogue again. This question also helps you understand the client's current challenges and whether or not you truly might be able to help them. Once you have listened to them, you can then give them a recent success story of how you have helped a client in a similar situation and what their results were. At that point, you will have caught their attention, and then you can say, "You know, it sounds like it might be worth sitting down at another time so I can better understand the full scope of your challenges and take the time to explain how our products/services will ensure you can reach _____ goal in your business. How does that sound?" Then ask for the appointment again!

Or, Get Creative!

Sometimes you have to get creative to secure the appointment. Now, let me be clear, I'm not advocating that you should be persistent unless you truly believe that you can solve their problem. Persistence will usually pay off with a client, but don't be persistent unless you know without a doubt that this is a prospect you want to work with. Sometimes this is hard to know until you meet with them in person, but just make sure that from your perspective the prospect is worth pursuing. If you have done your due diligence and definitely believe that they are a good fit, then you might want to add in some creativity to your sales process.

When I was in the IT Industry, I had an Account Executive who was extremely persistent. One day he came into my office and told me he was trying to connect with the Training

> As you let fear go, you are able to focus on all of the opportunities that you can now capture.

Manager at a large Fortune 500 company in Southern California. I asked him how many times he had tried to connect with her. A big smile formed on his face, he looked down, shook his head sheepishly, and said, "I don't know. I've lost count." In other words, he had left countless messages on her voicemail, and other countless times just calling her trying to get through, but he never made a connection. He looked at me and said, "I'm not giving up. There has to be a way."

We both agreed this could be a phenomenal account for him and an excellent target client, so I said, "Let's brainstorm." Thirty minutes later, he decided that he was going to send her a cactus plant with a card that read, "I don't mean to be a thorn in your side, but I really want to meet with you." He sent it that same day. And guess what? She called him within minutes of receiving the cactus and was ready to meet. Talk about an intentional connection! How persistent are you willing to be to land your target clients?

Now You Have the Appointment!

Now you have the appointment! Congratulations! But remember that your opportunity to earn this prospect's business is just beginning. There are several other tasks prior to your appointment that I would encourage you to do.

First, send them a hand written note, or e-mail, thanking them for agreeing to meet with you on said date. A note like that does two things. First, it confirms the appointment so they will be sure not to schedule something else during that time. Second, it shows them how professional you are. Remember, they are judging you and developing perceptions of you during this entire process, so you always need to put your most professional foot forward. Plus, people buy from sales people who are confident and know what they're doing. Let your confidence shine through how you interact with this client from the first time you meet through the rest of your relationship.

I want to emphasize a couple of final points. First, *stop questioning what you know*. Sales people often get in their own way by putting off making appointments because they question what they know and feel they need to know everything before they can talk to a prospect. That is simply not true! If a prospect asks you a question and you don't know the answer, tell them! Then tell them you are going to get their question answered from the expert in your company. It is a great reason to follow up and offer them great customer service from the beginning. You don't need to feel embarrassed because you don't know the answer. In fact, it will show your prospect more credibility if you tell them that you will get back to them with the RIGHT answer!

Finally, *be yourself.* I cannot stress this enough. People will sense if you are "putting on" or not acting like your true self. They might not pick up on it right away, but when you are faking something, eventually it will come out. When it comes out, it will only bring you challenges, and you will probably lose the client. When you are your true, authentic self, people will see you as human and like you even more. This is not to say that you should not be professional. *It means that you should be who you are.* Let your amazing qualities shine through to your prospects. Doing this alone will net you many new clients!

$ INTENTIONAL ACTION

Would you like to leave a powerful voicemail that gets prospects to call you back?

Check out www.SalesCoachNow.com to learn more!

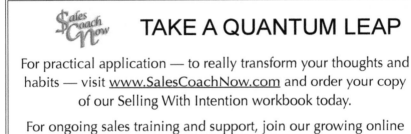

Ask for the Business

"You must do the thing you think you cannot do."

— Eleanor Roosevelt —

Closing Sales With Intention

Closing sales. Those two words can drum up feelings ranging from extreme excitement to panic. As we've discussed throughout *Selling with Intention, "selling"* just doesn't feel natural to most people, and closing a sale can feel even less natural. However, as seasoned sales professionals know, asking for the sale every time (as long as it is in the best interest of your prospect) is the only way to increase your sales. Sounds simple, and it can be, but you have to get out of your own way. Most people cannot make a decision to purchase your services unless you ask them to. But most of us just aren't asking for the business enough. We set out with great intentions. We set appointments. But in the end, even if we get the appointment (refer to Chapter 9), we never ask for the business.

Let's take it one step further: Closing sales with intention. What kind of feelings does this conjure up for you? What does it mean? *Closing sales with intention means you decide before you show up*

135

for the meeting that the prospect is going to become your new client because they fit your target client profile and you know you can solve their problem. You assume you are getting the sale.

Assuming the sale changes the entire conversation during the appointment. One of my colleagues quickly grew her business to over six figures the first year. When I asked her how she did it, she simply said, "I just assumed that every client I was going to meet with wanted to work with me. Isn't that what I was supposed to do?" Yes, it is, but most people lack that level of confidence.

Throughout the entire sales process, remember that confidence sells. Sometimes people won't even know why they are buying from you other than that they "like you" and "trust you". Prospects make buying decisions based on your confidence level, how much they like you, and whether or not they believe you can solve their problem. Let your confidence shine, and remember to be yourself and connect with intention.

Develop a List of Questions

Once you have scheduled the appointment, you can then focus on how you are going to close the sale. During the appointment, you need to have a clear presentation of your products or services developed, but that's not where you begin. You begin with a list of ten or more carefully crafted questions. The sales presentation, or sharing information about your products or services, follows your questions because only then can you decide which solutions to present based on the problems you believe you can solve for them.

> Most people cannot make a decision to purchase your services UNLESS YOU ASK THEM TO!

Here are some questions you may ask during your sales meeting:

- *What are the biggest challenges you are facing in your position (or with your company)?*
- *What are the top three projects you have on your plate right now?*
- *Where do you see your business (or department) two years from now?*
- *If you were to sign a contract with our company, what results would you like to achieve?*
- *When would you like to achieve _____ in your business?*
- *What is stopping you from moving forward right now?*
- *What will it take to earn your business?*

During your official appointment, continue to build rapport by actively listening to your prospect. Active listening will allow you to step into your prospect's world so you can truly understand what they are dealing with in their position or in their company. If they took the time to meet with you, they believe the product or service you offer has the potential to truly help them. Make sure you have exhausted all of the questions that you have for your prospect to get a clear understanding of what they really want. Only then will you be able to customize your product or services to best meet their needs.

During the meeting, you can begin to outline some possible solutions for them, but most of the time you will need to schedule another meeting to come back and present an official proposal (unless you are in a business that has limited products or services and doesn't require a proposal). Now some people will argue that if you have done your job, you should be able to close the business on a handshake. I agree with that to an extent. However, most savvy prospects and business people will ask for a written proposal to summarize the customized solutions that you have just described to them. I recommend at least three solutions for them to pick from.

The proposal will also include pricing, of course, and that is assumed by the prospect. A good sign that you have done your job, though, is when the prospect does not ask about price. If they haven't asked about price, it is because they believe that whatever the price, the investment will be worth the results they will receive.

One of my clients called me because he was really nervous about an upcoming appointment with a prospect. He told me that he was worried about coming across as "salesy" and didn't want to be perceived that way. I told him just to relax and focus his attention on connecting with the prospect and asking a lot of questions rather than "selling" him anything. After all, they were going to be meeting over lunch, and my guess was that the prospect really wanted to get a sense of what doing business with my client would be like.

Later my client shared that the lunch meeting started out kind of awkward because the prospect explained up front that he needed to get three quotes from three different companies and not to expect to get the business. However, by the end of the lunch appointment, the prospect liked (and trusted!) my client so much because of their authentic connection that he gave him all of the business and didn't even shop for two other proposals! Remember to always connect with intention throughout the sales process. I promise that you will get more sales!

Invite & Handle Objections

Whether you can close the sale at the first meeting or the second meeting, you need to invite and handle any objections that the prospect might have during your appointment. Now, if you have already connected with intention, then it is likely the prospect will openly share their objections with you because a level of trust has been created. Sometimes objections are just excuses, though, and may mask what the client is really thinking.

If the prospect tells you that their number one concern is money, then you need to delve deeper. Money is usually not the "real" concern. Prospects will always find the money if they want something desperately enough, or you could set up a payment plan that overcomes this objection. At this point in the sale, the real issues and questions that they might have are really related to the relationship that you have developed with them and whether or not you have demonstrated the value of the products or services you are offering.

Have you really connected with intention, or do they feel like you care only about closing the sale for your own personal financial benefit?

> Your proposal will reflect you, your business, and your services, so *every* detail counts!

Prospects need to know that you have their best interest in mind and are there to help them. If they sense anything else, the deal will be over.

If this is your first appointment and you need to write the proposal, explain that you need to set another appointment so you can go over it with them. This is your opportunity to shine! Remember, always under-promise and over-deliver. I'm sure you have heard that statement before because it is one of the most important things you can do to further develop rapport and trust with your client.

Some companies will require you to submit the proposal before the meeting. Give yourself enough time to write the proposal and deliver it before the date that you tell them you will. If you tell your prospect that you will deliver the proposal by Thursday, do everything in your power to deliver it Wednesday or even Tuesday. On top of delivering it early, it is extremely important that you deliver it with style. The proposal should be professionally bound and packaged. The content should be professionally laid out and spelling and grammar checks must be completed. Your proposal will reflect you, your business and your services, so every detail counts. Include a cover letter with the proposal that clearly lays out what the next steps will be. At a minimum, the cover letter should briefly summarize the proposal and what you discussed in addition to reminding the client when your next meeting will take place.

At the next in-person appointment, continue to assume that this opportunity is moving forward in your favor and begin to schedule the details including the start or delivery date. When you do this, you will draw out any final objections that your prospect might have. At this stage, final objections might really just be clarifications or opportunities for explanation, not deal breakers. So, don't worry. Just continue to connect with your prospect in the present moment, stay committed to their best interests, and you will soon have a new client!

One of my clients was in the middle of negotiating a large contract when she urgently texted me to tell me that the prospect wanted to revisit the terms of the agreement. My client panicked for a moment, but I reminded her that negotiating was just part of the sales process. You don't always get it right the first time in your proposal. Negotiating is just creating a solution that works well for your new client and for you. If a client wants to negotiate, just take a deep breath, continue to assume the sale and work out the best possible solution without giving away all of your profit. After all, companies are in business to turn a profit in addition to helping their clients.

Be willing to stay in the game as long as it takes. Statistically, it has been said that all of the major deals are closed after the third *no*. Are you willing to hear three *no's*, or do you run after the first one? If your prospect says *no*, then it is your opportunity to find out what you missed or what it would really take for them to be a client. It is okay to ask that question and find out what is really going on. You might say, "Thank you, Susie, for being willing to meet with me. It sounds like what I am offering isn't a fit for you. Could you please tell me what would need to be different for it to work for you?" That simple question can open up another dialogue with your prospect that could then lead to a closed sale. If you really want to help your prospects, then work closely with them throughout the sales process so you figure out what they really want. Decide that they will be a new client. Then deliver.

Perception is Reality

While juggling the many aspects of the sale that we have discussed in this chapter, you must also pay close attention to your 'inside' game — the one that goes on inside your head. We've already covered the importance of confidence during the sales process. The best way to manage your confidence level is to continue to be aware and manage your thoughts throughout the appointment.

There are days when even the most successful sales professionals in the world are lacking confidence, but they understand the importance of feeling that confidence again as quickly as possible. You, too, can change your inside world by, again, paying attention to what you are saying to yourself and taking control of the results you want to achieve by experiencing success in your mind first.

I'll show you what I mean with a visualization exercise that you can use before your next meeting.

💲 INTENTIONAL ACTION

The next time you are scheduled to meet with a client, knowing that you have the opportunity to close the sale, I want you to take the time and the space prior to the meeting to go through the following visualization.

First, close your eyes and imagine that you have already closed the sale. Get in touch with what that feels like inside. Then make that feeling ten times stronger (you might feel excited, more confident, etc.)! Next, visualize the room and the people around you. Notice how they look. Check in and add smiles to their faces. See them thrilled about the opportunity to purchase your products or services. Watch them as they sign the contract. Then, imagine that you have stepped outside yourself. Take a look at your face. See a calm, confident, and professional look on your face.

Then, still standing in the future when you closed the sale, in your mind's eye, imagine that there is a timeline in front of you. Look at that timeline and watch everything that happened from the moment that you walked into the building all the way to the second your client signed the paperwork. Notice exactly how it played out.

Change anything that you don't like and then let the entire sequence play out again. You are programming your brain to support you in an amazing way because you have already chosen the results that you want to achieve with the client!

Magic? Not at all.

The power of visualization has been proven by sports professionals around the world, so take advantage of it!

Perception is reality, so when you visualize a successful close ahead of time, you are going to be confident and successful during a client meeting, your brain will support you in that reality, and you will emanate confidence to your clients. Even more importantly, your clients will sense your confidence, and since you have already played out the entire scenario in your head, they will typically react with that same confidence in you! When they feel confident in you, they will want to do business with you and you will close the sale.

The Deal Is Never Over

In 1998, I was promoted to Branch Manager and asked to take on a branch that was losing $60,000 per month. When my manager asked me how soon I could bring the branch to a "break even" level, I told him two months. I remember that after it came out of my mouth, I wanted to take it back. But he agreed that the two months was the right amount of time. At that point, I was a selling branch manager, a position that I truly enjoyed, but it added a lot of pressure to my job since I was also in charge of a full staff. In order to reach that goal of break even, I knew that I had to close a large deal.

When I arrived at the new branch, I was told about a deal that was on the table with an international firm located close to the office. When I went over the deal with the sales person, I realized two very important things. One, the deal was going to lose us a lot of money. Two, the client would be very unhappy in the end because we would not be able to properly deliver the services at that price point. This was going to prove to be a huge dilemma.

The sales person who had been working on this account moved on from the company about a week later, so I was left with a rather large mess, and the thought of going in and telling this client that we could not deliver the project based on the numbers he had already been given was quite intimidating. However, I knew that I had to do it and do it fast because the financial health of the branch depended on me. People's jobs depended on this deal. I knew the stakes.

I set an emergency meeting with the client. My intention was to explain to the client that the only way we could deliver this business was to increase the cost by approximately 40%. I knew this would be a significant increase, but it was the only way we could deliver a quality product.

> If you lead with integrity and quality, the rest will work itself out because it is truly never about the money.

On top of that, I was also going to need to ask the client to pay for a project manager to ensure that a project of this magnitude would be delivered without a glitch. Our IT training would be piggy-backing on the delivery of technology to every one of their two hundred branches across the United States. So, timing would be essential and the project manager would have to carefully manage the process.

After a tense phone call, the client agreed to meet with me. I sat down across from the client and explained that the original quote he had been given was wrong. I told him that the Account Executive was no longer with the company, and that I, the Branch Manager, was now personally handling this account. I saw the blood quickly rise up through his face and knew that his response was not going to be a happy one. I continued to explain that if he wanted us to deliver high-quality IT training, a delivery that would piggy-back perfectly on the delivery of the software, he needed to trust my experience and what I was telling him. The additional fees would ensure that we utilized top trainers and an excellent project manager. His face was really, really red. He proceeded to read me the riot act.

I sat there and listened. I wish I could say that I was completely calm, but that would be a lie. My heart was in my throat. After he was done with his tirade, he stopped and took a deep breath. I remained silent because I knew that the next words that were going to come out of his mouth would be some of the most important I would ever hear him say about this project. He explained that this delivery had to be perfect. He only delivered quality projects in his department, and if he had to pay more to properly deliver this project, he would. Okay, it wasn't *exactly* like that, but basically. He then told me to get him the numbers (the official proposal) by the next day so he could give them final approval because the project started Monday. He expected my project manager to be there Monday morning.

I sweated bullets throughout the next four months during the delivery of the project. There were many glitches along the way (it was a difficult and complex venture), but because I had a phenomenal project manager on board, everything was still delivered on time. Every trainer knew what was riding on this mission, and they all stepped up to the plate. At the end of the project, our company won an award for excellence. I still keep the certificate of recognition close by as a reminder of the importance of keeping the client's best interest in mind when closing a sale. If you lead with integrity and quality, the rest will work itself out because it is truly never about the money.

To summarize, remember to always do what is in the best interest of your client and ask for the business like your job or your company depends on it. In most cases, your job does depend on your ability to close sales! Give 100% to connecting with intention, love your clients, and the results will speak for themselves!

PART II

Special Bonus Section

Take A Quantum Leap —

With Intention!

Design Your Own Quantum Leap

"Do not wait; the time will never be 'just right'. Start where you stand, and work with whatever tools you may have at your command, and better tools will be found as you go along."

— Napoleon Hill —

Are you Ready?

*T*aking this journey with you has been a true honor! Now that you have experienced the ten principles of *Selling With Intention*, I hope that you are feeling excited about the opportunity to significantly increase your sales this year! For some of you, 10% will be enough because of the size of your business or the time you have available to dedicate to selling. Others picked up this book because they want to double or even triple their sales this year. I added this bonus section for you — those of you who truly want to make a serious increase in your sales this year and desire a little extra help. This bonus section is designed to take you deeper in every area of selling.

If you are not ready to take a quantum leap this year, that's okay! It is best if you understand how much you really want to stretch yourself and when the timing would be just right. However, I want to caution you to not confuse fear of the unknown with *"bad timing"*. Fear is a reaction that flows from our ego to keep us safe from harm, but at the same time, it can stop us from reaching our true potential in sales if we allow it. My purpose is to help sales people and entrepreneurs take a quantum leap in selling so they can give back to the world in their own unique way. That is what motivates me to help you stretch to the next level. I know you have great financial plans — both to enjoy life and to give back!

What is a Quantum Leap?

A quantum leap, according to The *American Heritage Dictionary*, is defined as, *"An abrupt change or step, especially in method, information, or knowledge."* In sales, a quantum leap is simply a *giant* step from where you are right now, but it looks different for everyone. It means you have stopped taking small, incremental steps toward your sales goals, and you are now choosing a quantum leap.

A quantum leap might mean that you have been averaging $25,000.00 per month in sales, and instead of just taking a small step to $30,000.00 per month, you have decided to double your sales to $50,000.00 per month. For someone else, it might mean that your company had revenues of $500,000.00 last year, but this year, you have decided that you want to reach $2,000,000.00. That is a quantum leap!

My first quantum leap happened when I didn't even understand what a quantum leap was! They say that ignorance is bliss and, in this case, I really believe it because not knowing what was happening made it easier. I didn't get in my own way because I just stayed focused on the goal that the team had set, and collectively we kept taking steps toward it.

One of the Sales Teams that I worked with allowed me to experience leading a quantum leap and to be there as it unfolded. When I first began working with them, they were averaging $25,000.00 to $50,000.00 per month in sales. One day I asked them what it would take to go from $50,000.00 to $100,000.00 per month. What was amazing was that they had an answer. They knew they could take a quantum leap by working with larger, different clients and by creating and selling different packages and classes. It was amazing to see how quickly they figured out a way to reach that goal with only a question to generate the plan!

> Reaching a goal as a group can be much easier than reaching one alone. In my own experience, I have found that a Mastermind Group can be a powerful way to keep you focused and on track!

Over the next couple of years, we kept asking that question and raising the sales goal as they kept reaching it. They were reaching unbelievable numbers of $500,000.00 per month and beyond (per person)! What I learned from that experience is that you cannot have a quantum leap in your sales until you begin to ask yourself what it would take to double or even triple your sales. You have to ask the question! The best part is that we did it using a simple excel spreadsheet to track their progress.

$ INTENTIONAL ACTION

What would it take for you to double or triple your sales?

It's Not About You

The people I have seen become the most successful have also helped a lot of other people become successful along the way. They did this in a variety of ways including being excellent leaders and helping others succeed whenever they could, as well as by helping others reach their goals through the products and services they offered.

When I first started my career as a sales professional, I was filled with fear and limiting beliefs. As I would pick up the telephone to make a call, I was paralyzed with thoughts about what the prospect on the other end might be thinking. "What if they think I am pushy?" I would ask myself, feeling my stomach turn over. And then they would answer, and I would stumble over my words, getting all caught up in thoughts of failure and knowing that I would never land this client. Not in a million years! Who would want to do business with such a bumbling idiot?

And then I realized something.

It wasn't about me. As much as I wanted to believe that I had to be the perfect sales person to sell something, I started to realize that it really wasn't about me. The prospect on the other end of the line wasn't going to waste their time thinking about whether or not I was a good sales person. They had their mind on a million other things that they were dealing with in their personal or professional life.

It wasn't about me; it was about them. Either I could solve their problem and make a difference for them, or I couldn't. It was that simple. If I could, then I could ask for an appointment to understand some of the challenges they were facing and whether or not we could at least meet to see if my product or service could help them. Isn't that freeing? I had become a sales person who knew that my job was to get an appointment, meet with my prospect, and determine whether or not I could help them. *And that changed everything.*

> To make a Quantum Leap in sales, you have to continually remind yourself that it's not about you.

Fears that I had carried around for years just disappeared because now I was on a mission to help as many people as possible with my products and services. I was no longer caught up in the worry of being rejected. Instead, I was focused on solving problems, and I gave off a much different energy that made others want to connect with me and, ultimately, buy my services.

Someone once said that when you get better, your clients will get better too. In order to "be" that person who has made a quantum leap, it is critical that you do the *internal work* as well as the *external "actions"* ahead of time. As I demonstrated earlier in this book, it is important to choose what you want and actively set your plan in motion, and then "listen for" the inspired and intentional ideas that come to you. The internal journey is taken by continuing to explore your limiting beliefs and fears that are preventing you from reaching your goals. As you consciously continue to release them, you will feel an energy that will make you unstoppable in your sales!

Acknowledge Your Financial Comfort Zone

Have you ever noticed that no matter how hard you try to surpass it, you reach the same sales amount every month? In my experience, I have found that most sales people and entrepreneurs have a *financial set point* that they keep bumping up against. I find that it is often like weight. With weight, your body naturally returns to where it is most comfortable. It is the same for your financial set point. You keep returning to the financial level that feels the most comfortable for you. It is possible to change your financial set point, but you have to become aware of it first and then begin to change your behavior so you can get better results.

To adjust your financial set point, you also need to choose a number that is *believable* to you. Others may want to influence you in this area, but spend time finding a sales goal that feels like a stretch, but still feels achievable. It should also feel slightly out of your comfort zone. Start by looking back at the past six months of your results to find your financial set point. Are

> As you consciously continue to release your fears and limiting beliefs, you will feel an energy that will make you unstoppable in your sales!

you typically selling $20,000.00 per month consistently or are you reaching $50,000.00 per month? If you consistently reach $50,000.00 per month in sales, then that is your financial set point. By recognizing that first, you can then move toward changing it.

Your financial set point is often your "Survival Mode". In other words, every month you are just reaching the sales goal that you know allows you to pay all of your bills but doesn't allow you to pay your debt off or contribute to your savings. That is simply not the goal you want to stay focused on! Even though we all know this, sometimes we just stay in that space because it is comfortable.

Now that you know what your set point is, it is up to you to make the commitment to yourself to reach your stretch goal so that you can begin to make the impact on the world that you know you can! The good news is that you can change your financial set point. The way to change it is to change the way you think about a month. At the beginning of the month, your sense of urgency to sell is low. To change your set point, increase your sense of urgency early in the month by getting sales in the first week. Your confidence will build and you will naturally close more sales and change your set point!

When I first began to understand the financial set point, I tested the idea with a sales team I was working with. What we found was that when the sales team members sold their services the first week of the month, they were often able to reach their stretch goal for the month. When they didn't, they often reached their financial set point.

When you are aware of your financial set point, you can make an impact on your sales early in the month and break through your comfort zone, ultimately taking a quantum leap!

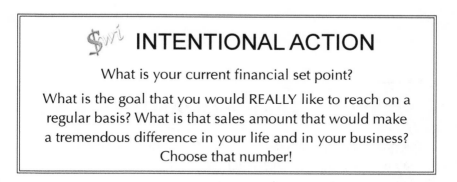

$ INTENTIONAL ACTION

What is your current financial set point?

What is the goal that you would REALLY like to reach on a regular basis? What is that sales amount that would make a tremendous difference in your life and in your business? Choose that number!

TAKE A QUANTUM LEAP

For practical application — to really transform your thoughts and habits — visit www.SalesCoachNow.com and order your copy of our Selling With Intention workbook today.

For ongoing sales training and support, join our growing online community at www.MySalesCoachNow.com.

Take a Quantum Leap — With Intention

"Never, Never, Never Give Up."

— Winston Churchill —

Take Your Own Quantum Leap

*T*aking a quantum leap can transform your sales career or your business and, ultimately, your life. It is important to take your time with each step so that you can move through the process intentionally and release any limiting beliefs or fears that you may have before you move to the next level. For some of you, a quantum leap might mean that you could double or even triple your business by just adding three new clients. For others, taking a quantum leap could mean adding ten new clients or repackaging your products or services in a new way. Whatever it is for you, just know that you are reading this for a reason, and this is perfect timing for you. Some of you could actually take a quantum leap in your sales and increase your business today by simply making one or two phone calls and scheduling just one or two new appointments. If this makes your heart beat faster, then I am talking to you!

5 Steps to Take a Quantum Leap — With Intention!

From my experience in achieving and facilitating quantum leaps, I have created a five-step formula designed to make it easier for you to take one yourself. If you get stuck along the way, simply go back to first step and release any beliefs or fears that you need to let go of.

First Step: *Shift Your Belief*

The first step in taking a quantum leap is to shift your belief about what it means to be a sales person. Even if you are an entrepreneur, you still need to be the best sales person on your team because if you can't sell your products or services, it will be hard for other people to sell them. Often, when I first connect with sales professionals and entrepreneurs, I find that they have very negative beliefs about what it means to be a sales professional. And when I tell my clients that they don't have to be a sales person, they just look at me funny. But the truth is, when you shift your belief about what it means to be a sales person, you truly don't have to think of yourself in a negative light anymore.

 INTENTIONAL ACTION

Check your beliefs again about what it means to be a sales person. Is there anything else that you need to shift so you can more easily move forward?

So if you aren't a sales person, then what *are* you? The simple answer is that *you are a problem-solver*. You solve the problems of your clients so that they can move forward in their business in whatever way they need to. Selling no longer feels "bad" when you are connecting with intention, creating a relationship with a prospect with the goal of figuring out whether or not you can help them. If you can, great; if not, then you are ready to refer them to someone else who can.

One way to shift this belief in a big way is to begin telling a new story to prospects, clients and strategic business partners. This new story is about the problems that you have solved for your clients and your goal to help new clients solve their problems as well.

$wi INTENTIONAL ACTION

Take out a piece of paper and write at least one paragraph regarding the way in which you solve problems for your clients.

THIS is the story that you need to begin to tell!

Second Step: *Set a Quantum Goal*

Whenever I begin working with a client to help them take a quantum leap, I always ask them what "their numbers are". In other words, I want to know what they have been averaging in their sales results every month and what it would mean for them to take a quantum leap. Remember, a quantum leap in sales is going to be different for everyone so it is important to choose numbers that work best for you.

It's also important for me to know why they want to take a Quantum Leap. Usually, if it just to "get more things" or "have more money", that's not enough to catapult them. However, if it is to help even more people and businesses with the product or service they offer, then I know that they are well on their way!

When you set a quantum goal, or a stretch goal, you will allow yourself to see opportunities that you didn't even know were there. In my previous example about the IT Training industry, the higher we set our goals, the more we were able to see opportunities that we didn't even know had existed! When you are crystal clear about what your stretch goal is, you will give your goal even more energy and power.

Then, ask yourself, *What is* the fastest *and* easiest *way to take my own quantum leap?* Have fun with this! I recommend that you ask this question with a trusted accountability partner, mentor or mastermind member, and write down at least twenty ideas. Then, take action on those ideas and watch what unfolds!

$wi **INTENTIONAL ACTION**

Set the quantum goal here by asking, "What is the fastest and easiest way to reach my quantum goal?"

Third Step: *Be Accountable and Supported*

No matter what, do not try to do this on your own! I cannot stress this enough, but you *must* have a support team around you in order to make your quantum leap. Sure, you could probably do it on your own, but it will be much more difficult. With a support team around you to help hold you accountable, it will be much easier. If you feel like you don't have anyone around you who supports you, then it's time to form a support team for yourself.

Building a support team took me awhile. I was used to doing things on my own and just putting my head down and working. But as I added more friends, colleagues, mentors and staff to my personal advisory board, things just kept getting easier. You need to have people to support you in your professional life as well as in your personal life.

One of the most powerful steps I took was joining a Mastermind Group. This was a group that I invested heavily in (financially, emotionally, and time), not just a group of people who decided to get together one day. In my experience, investing in a Mastermind Group can make a huge difference for you. I feel so strongly about it that I created a program for my own clients called *Sales Coach*

> When you connect your sales goals with your Soul Purpose, or your ability to make a difference, you become unstoppable! Please note that you can be selling anything and still be making an incredible difference for people and businesses.

Now Quantum Leap, and it has been instrumental in helping my clients move forward quickly in their businesses! You can learn more by visiting *www.SalesCoachNow.com* if you are in need of that type of support.

The other benefit of having a coach or being in a Mastermind Group is that they can help you energetically leap to the next level. Napoleon Hill, author of the classic *Think and Grow Rich*, created and explained the idea of the Mastermind Group in the early 1900's: "The coordination of knowledge and effort of two or more people, who work toward a definite purpose, in the spirit of harmony." And then he added, "No two minds ever come together without thereby creating a third, invisible intangible force, which may be likened to a third mind." After reading and studying his material, I realized that I just HAD to find a Mastermind Group that I could join. You can significantly decrease the amount of time it takes you to make a quantum leap by being connected to those professionals who are where you want to be. Be open and be a sponge to what they are willing to teach you, and you will soon find yourself on a high-speed train racing toward your goals!

Another way to stay accountable to your goals is through sales tracking. If you aren't tracking your prospects and closed sales yet, don't panic, but make a commitment to yourself that you will begin. At a minimum, you need a simple excel spreadsheet to track your prospects, 99% closed, and closed sales. There are more sophisticated Customer Relationship Management Systems out there that can also help you track your sales. Find the software and system that will work best for you.

💲 INTENTIONAL ACTION

Who is on your support team? Who would you like to add?

Fourth Step: *Be Open to Receive*

Even with all of the good work above, if you aren't open to receive, none of it will matter. For money to flow freely to you, you must be interested in solving your clients' problems and be open to receiving their money or commission. In fact, if you give your services away (or deeply discount them) without receiving compensation, you are actually doing a disservice to your clients. I have noticed that the more clients pay me, the more results they experience for themselves because they are even more motivated. Ask to be paid what your products or services are worth and then gratefully receive the money.

> One of my favorite books about money and abundance is *Money and The Law of Attraction* by Jerry and Esther Hicks. They have a simple way of teaching how the Law of Attraction works and especially how you can apply it to allowing more money and abundance to come into your life.

A simple way to examine your receiving abilities is to notice your ability to receive a simple compliment. When someone gives you a compliment, how well do you receive it? Or, do you just brush it off? Begin practicing accepting compliments with gratitude and grace, and you will be amazed at how that will translate to your ability to accept the financial abundance that is available to flow to you at any time.

Finally, whenever you receive a new sale or close a deal, feel the gratitude! Being grateful can keep you motivated and excited about what you are doing. If you don't stop and take time to acknowledge all of the sales that are coming to you, they just might stop coming so quickly. Practicing gratitude on a daily basis can make what you do even more enjoyable on every level.

$ⱳᶦ INTENTIONAL ACTION

Do you feel like you are open to receiving all of the sales and abundance that is available to you?

If not, what do you have to shift to feel that way?

Fifth Step: *Make a Commitment to Yourself…And to Your Target Clients*

Commitment is defined as, *"The state of being bound emotionally or intellectually to a course of action or to another person or persons"* according to the *American Heritage Dictionary.* When you make a commitment to yourself, think of it almost like a marriage. Marriage is a big commitment: You form a contract with another human being. This commitment is a contract with yourself, and you are telling the world that you are truly committed to making a quantum leap in your business, no matter what.

When you make taking a quantum leap a priority, it is also important to create an intentional schedule that supports this commitment. Your schedule MUST be set up to reach your stretch goals. In addition, it is important to schedule ample time to follow up with your prospects. Refer back to the Intentional Schedule and Follow-Up chapters if you need to review this portion.

When I launched *Sales Coach Now*, I made a contract and commitment with myself that I would launch it thirty days later at a live launch event. The commitment was even made public because

I had invited hundreds of people to the event. Until I was really committed and had made this public announcement, I wasn't on my way to taking a quantum leap.

You also need to make a commitment to yourself to let go of those things that no longer serve you. Entrepreneurs and sales professionals typically love to give back and volunteer their time. This is great as long as you keep it in check. I know I might be sending a mixed message here because I teach people to sell more so they can give back to the organizations they care about, but there are more ways to give back than just with your time. Part of your goal might be to give back *financially* which doesn't involve more of your time. Remember that when you move on from a volunteer leadership role, you also make room for someone else to take that on and to grow. Moving on is giving a gift to the next person.

Finally, make a commitment to always do the right thing for your prospects and clients. By keeping their best interest in mind, you will always win.

 ## INTENTIONAL ACTION

Take a moment right now and write down all of the organizations that you give your time back to.

Again, it is not to stop being involved with these organizations or to stop supporting them. But are there some that you could shift from giving time to giving a financial gift instead and still make an impact?

Because I know that success in sales and business requires the highest levels of determination and commitment, I have created a sample commitment form and included it here for you. If you need to rewrite it in your own words or add specific details, please feel free to do so.

Refer to this commitment when you want to take your business to the next level and need a good starting point, or when you feel tired or like you have lost your way. The most successful sales professionals and entrepreneurs thrive because they constantly revisit their commitments to themselves, their businesses, and their clients, and make sure their behavior and business are aligned with those.

My Commitment

I commit to being a Problem-Solver — to making calls, going to networking events, and setting appointments in order to find out if my products/services truly can help my prospects with the challenges they are facing.

I commit to making a Quantum Leap in my sales — to leap from making $_____ every month (my current Financial Set Point) to my Quantum Leap Goal of $_____ per month by _____ (Goal Achievement Date).

I commit to surrounding myself with people who can support me and keep me accountable as I move toward my goals, and I commit to tracking my progress.

I commit to being more and more open to receiving everything that I need to reach my Quantum Leap Goal — the target clients, the support from accountability partners, inspired ideas, etc.

I commit to being open to gratefully receiving the abundance that will flow to me as I move toward and achieve my Quantum Goal.

I commit to staying in tune with myself and releasing the limiting beliefs and fears as I discover them.

I commit to NOT LETTING ANYTHING STOP ME from achieving my goals so that I can do what I want to do in this world — enjoy my life and give back!

Your Signature _____

Don't Let Anything Stop You

Once you have made a commitment to yourself to take a quantum leap in your sales, don't let anything stop you! Things will come up that could potentially take you off track, but it is up to you to stay committed and implement all of the mindset, tools, and strategies you have learned in this book. It takes all of them to move at quantum leap speed!

Taking a quantum leap should not feel stressful or "bad". If it does, begin with Step 1 again because it means that you haven't cleared out a limiting belief or fear that has been stopping you from moving forward. If you need to go deeper in this area, I recommend finding someone who can help you address these issues. Most importantly, taking a quantum leap should be fun, and you should feel great along the way.

I have seen many people get caught up in one or the other. They work really hard on implementing all of the tools — the intentional schedule, the follow-up, the tracking process, etc. — but they do not consistently pay attention to and release the negative self-talk and beliefs that continue to sabotage their efforts.

Others work through the negative self-talk and limiting beliefs but do not implement the systems and tools that would allow them to change their sales results at a quantum speed.

If you want results, you must do the hard work — on your inner world and your outer world. I believe that there are times when we need to quickly take the intentional steps that are being presented to us, and that can "feel" like hard work. When we launched *My Sales Coach Now* and I set the launch date thirty days after we started working on building the membership community, the date out there (publicly) put my actions into high gear, and I didn't have a choice but to push through each day. Believe me, there were days when I was tired and would have rather been doing something else, but because I had set the date I knew that I had to finish it. I took breaks when I needed them, but I just kept pushing, and we reached our deadline just days before our live launch in front of one hundred people!

> Understand the Power of Intention in your Sales Process (this can change EVERYTHING!) and review the 10 Principles of Selling with Intention whenever you feel stuck. Commit to working with only your target clients, and don't waste your time on those who will only drain your time and your energy.

Once you release your limiting beliefs and start moving toward your quantum leap goals, you will begin to feel the "flow". The "flow" feels good and you know it is happening because all of your needs are met and extra abundance and opportunities just seem to be flowing easily to you! We've all been there at one time or another, but I want you to begin to believe that you can stay in that place of flow simply by staying focused on what you want, feeling good, and continuing to release those things that no longer serve you.

There might be days when you feel like giving up, but I want to encourage you to stay on the path of creating a quantum leap for yourself. You deserve it! Keep believing in yourself and remember that the world needs you to take that quantum leap so you can make your unique impact and leave your legacy!

Thanks again for allowing me the honor to take this journey with you. It has been my deepest pleasure, and I am filled with gratitude!

About the Author

Ursula Mentjes, sought after motivational speaker and Certified Sales Coach, has trained thousands of Sales Professionals and Entrepreneurs, helping many to double and triple their sales revenue. Ursula honed her sales and executive management skills at an International Technical Training company where she advanced to the position of President in just five years when she was 27 years old and the company's annual revenue was in the tens of millions. In 2004, Ursula launched her own sales coaching and training company that specializes in working with Entrepreneurs and Sales Professionals.

Ursula holds a Bachelor of Arts Degree in Psychology and Communication and a Master of Science Degree in Psychology. She is a Certified NLP Coach through the NLP Institute of California, and an Associate Certified Coach through the International Coach Federation. Ursula is Past President of the National Association of Women Business Owners Inland Empire Chapter, Past President of the Inland Empire Women's Education Foundation, Vice-President of Economic Development for the National Association of Women Business Owners of California, a founding member of the Business Resource Connection and the Director of Education, a 2006 Graduate of Leadership California, a 2007 Spirit of the Entrepreneur Finalist, named one of 951 Magazine's *51 to Watch* in 2008, and the recipient of the 2009 NAWBO-IE A.N.I.T.A. Award. She also serves on several non-profit boards that are near and dear to her heart.

Ursula C. Mentjes, M.S., ACC
Founder of Sales Coach Now
www.SalesCoachNow.com
www.MySalesCoachNow.com
Contact@SalesCoachNow.com

A Special Invitation from Ursula

FREE 30-Day Membership on *My Sales Coach Now*!

Imagine that selling could be fun, easy, AND exciting…

If you are ready to get started with ongoing training and support on the Principles of *Selling With Intention* — you don't have to wait!

We have designed a unique, virtual sales coaching and training community — *My Sales Coach Now* — that allows you to have instant access to the sales support you need — when you need it!

You can join at any time by visiting
www.MySalesCoachNow.com

If you would like to experience the program FREE for 30 days, just e-mail us directly at *Contact@SalesCoachNow.com* with "30 Days Free" in the subject line and we will set up your FREE account! In addition to the training and support, you will also be able to set up your profile so that other Sales Coach Now Members will be able to connect with you. Don't wait! This is the answer you've been looking for!

Client Success Story

"Before SCN, I was fearful and very intimidated of selling. After taking advantage of SCN's amazing introductory price and making my way through the $WI Training, I found out that I AM a sales person after all! Who knew?! I followed the Principles of *Selling With Intention* listed in the $WI Training step-by-step and IMMEDIATELY saw results!

I was able to overcome my initial fear of selling, define my target clients, focus on setting up capabilities with them and landed a meeting and first order with my #1 Target Client! SCN has shown me that selling is easy! It's just a matter of scheduling the time and asking the right questions. Thank you so much! Your services have proven to be invaluable to my development in sales. Thank you *Sales Coach Now*!!"

— **Mary Sanchez, Think Ink,** *www.thinkinkinfo.com*

If you desire more intensive training or support, then visit *www.SalesCoachNow.com* to learn more about our *Sales Coach Now* Quantum Leap Program as well as our *Selling With Intention* Intensive Courses.

While you are on the Sales Coach Now home page, please sign up for our FREE Monthly E-Zine and updates: "Where Mindset Meets Intention".

As our special gift to you, you will also receive the MP3 Download "7 Ways to Sell More in a Doom and Gloom Economy" just for signing up!

10% of the proceeds are donated to the Inland Empire Women's Business Center to help women and men launch and grow their businesses.

BUY A SHARE OF THE FUTURE IN YOUR COMMUNITY

These certificates make great holiday, graduation and birthday gifts that can be personalized with the recipient's name. The cost of one S.H.A.R.E. or one square foot is $54.17. The personalized certificate is suitable for framing and will state the number of shares purchased and the amount of each share, as well as the recipient's name. The home that you participate in "building" will last for many years and will continue to grow in value.

Here is a sample SHARE certificate:

HABITAT FOR HUMANITY

THIS CERTIFIES THAT

YOUR NAME HERE

HAS INVESTED IN A HOME FOR A DESERVING FAMILY

1985-2005

TWENTY YEARS OF BUILDING FUTURES IN OUR
COMMUNITY ONE HOME AT A TIME

1200 SQUARE FOOT HOUSE @ $65,000 = $54.17 PER SQUARE FOOT
This certificate represents a tax deductible donation. It has no cash value.

YES, I WOULD LIKE TO HELP!

I support the work that Habitat for Humanity does and I want to be part of the excitement! As a donor, I will receive periodic updates on your construction activities but, more importantly, I know my gift will help a family in our community realize the dream of homeownership. **I would like to SHARE in your efforts against substandard housing in my community!** *(Please print below)*

PLEASE SEND ME _____ SHARES at $54.17 EACH = $ $_____

In Honor Of: _____

Occasion: (Circle One)   HOLIDAY   BIRTHDAY   ANNIVERSARY

OTHER: _____

Address of Recipient: _____

Gift From: _____ *Donor Address:* _____

Donor Email: _____

I AM ENCLOSING A CHECK FOR $ $_____ PAYABLE TO HABITAT FOR HUMANITY <u>OR</u> PLEASE CHARGE MY VISA OR MASTERCARD *(CIRCLE ONE)*

Card Number _____ Expiration Date: _____

Name as it appears on Credit Card _____ Charge Amount $ _____

Signature _____

Billing Address _____

Telephone # Day _____ Eve _____

PLEASE NOTE: Your contribution is tax-deductible to the fullest extent allowed by law.
Habitat for Humanity • P.O. Box 1443 • Newport News, VA 23601 • 757-596-5553
www.HelpHabitatforHumanity.org

CPSIA information can be obtained
at www.ICGtesting.com
Printed in the USA
LVHW03s0535091018
592876LV00001B/1/P

9 781600 378416